D1564036

THE PALESTINE
LIBERATION ORGANIZATION:
ITS FUNCTION AND STRUCTURE

Dr. Sami Musallam

AMANA BOOKS
58 Elliot Street
Brattleboro, Vermont 05301

DS
119.7
.M8373
M87
1988

THE PALESTINE LIBERATION ORGANIZATION:
ITS FUNCTION AND STRUCTURE

CONTENTS

IN MEMORY of the Palestinian freedom fighters who lost their lives in the October 1, 1985, Israeli air raid on the PLO headquarters in Hamman al-Shatt, Tunisia.

INTRODUCTION

The purpose of this study is to explain the infrastructure and development of the Palestine Liberation Organization (PLO) by analyzing its institutional makeup which, despite great odds against it, has maintained the survival and continuation of the Palestine national movement and earned the PLO political stature within the international community. From its inception in 1964, the PLO has been subject to continuous attempts to eliminate its institutional framework and objectives. Over the years, these attempts have taken the form of open military and political warfare from Israel, consecutive U.S. administrations, certain Arab regimes, and even from dissidents within the Palestinian community. Opponents of the PLO have individually and collectively attempted to drive the PLO from the Middle East political equation. The Chairman of the PLO, Yasser Arafat, frequently asserts that the PLO is the most enigmatic figure in the Arab-Israeli conflict. Thus, to its opponents, the elimination of the PLO is requisite for the elimination of Palestinian national aspirations.

Although opposition to the PLO has taken many forms over the years, its main focus remains the physical elimination of Palestinian leadership, which, in the minds of many, will result in the destruction of the PLO's infrastructure. However, this view fails to take into consideration the internal and external dimensions of the PLO. These dimensions are detailed in the chapters which follow.

In the summer of 1982, Israel declared that one of its major objectives in invading Lebanon was the destruction of the infrastructure of the PLO.[1] Failing to achieve this objective, Israeli military leaders were not discouraged. They tried again on October 1, 1985,

1

by bombing the headquarters of the PLO in Hammam al-Shatt, in the southern suburbs of the Tunisian capital. The Israeli attack was clearly directed at assassinating Yasser Arafat in the hope that his demise would not only end the February 1985 joint Jordanian-Palestinian peace process initiative, but would also eliminate the PLO as an effective and credible actor on the Palestinian, Arab and international scenes.

Israel, of course, is not the sole opponent of the Palestinian national movement. Successive U.S. administrations have continuously patronized Israel politically, diplomatically, militarily and financially. Unquestioned U.S. support of Israel, as well as American refusal to recognize the national rights of the Palestinian people, have helped create a climate of disrespect and derision for the United States in the international community.

Despite near-universal recognition of the PLO as the legitimate representative entity of the Palestinian people, the United States government has never recognized the unanimous 1974 Rabat Arab summit resolution stating the unequivocal status of the PLO.

An observation of recent U.S. administration positions regarding the Palestinians and the PLO is illuminating. During the Nixon and Ford presidencies, Henry Kissinger implemented the U.S. policy of no dialogue with the PLO. Zbigniew Brezinski, national security advisor to President Carter, captured headlines with his "bye-bye PLO' statement.[2] And George Shultz, the current U.S. secretary of state, has unabashedly called upon the Arab states to withdraw their recognition of the PLO and rebuked them for their "mistakes."[3]

Within the Arab world, opponents of the PLO have reacted with fear and hostility to the PLO's institutionalization and national objectives. Throughout the 1970s and early 1980s, the PLO was subjected by several Arab states to threats of physical and political annihilation if it refused to fall in line with the established policies of regimes hosting Palestinian communities. A pseudo-alternative to the PLO was actually created — the so- called National Salvation Front in Damascus. Despite its being stillborn, and the failure of other Arab nations' attempts to remove or replace the PLO, the lesson was not learned that the Palestinian people had affirmed the PLO as their sole, legitimate representative.

THE FORMATIVE YEARS

The intensity of these efforts to destroy the PLO, and their failure, illustrates the inherent stability and commitment of Palestinians to the PLO.

Prior to the establishment of the PLO in 1964, the Palestinian people were deprived of nearly all forms of national expression or an independent, organized structure that fulfilled their economic, cultural, social, educational and informational needs. The terms "Palestinian nationalism" or "independent Palestinian expression" were for all practical purposes nonexistent. There did not exist a vehicle for Palestinian identity among the Palestinians nor at the Arab and international levels.

At the time, the "question of Palestine" had long been shelved from the agenda of the United Nations by the United States, its western allies and by then-U.N. Secretary-General Trygvie Lie, and replaced by the "Middle East situation."[4] More recently, during his much-publicized tour of Western European countries in January 1986, the then- Israeli Prime Minister, Shimon Peres, proposed to the Palestinian people the choice of either coming to peace negotiations without the PLO, or their exclusion from such talks, i.e., the continuation of living under occupation. Peres stated, "the Palestinian people have to choose the easiest of two things: the PLO without a solution, or a solution without the PLO."[5]

The U.N. and Peres examples above are indicative of efforts to silence Palestinian national expression and the fulfillment of Palestinian objectives. However, the achievements of the PLO and its development over 24 years from a position of weakness to that of strength cannot be reversed. Despite past and present moves to deny its legitimacy, the PLO has confirmed itself as the sole representative of the Palestinian people. The PLO earned this status because it has

3

established the framework within which every Palestinian can turn to receive protection and fulfill the needs for national identification.

This is especially important when one considers that today more than half of the Palestinian people live under Israeli occupation. They are Palestinians who do not enjoy freedom of political, social or economic expression, nor are their needs for informational, educational and security institutions fulfilled when their lives are determined by an occupational force.

Since its establishment, the PLO has transformed itself from an organization competing for Palestinian allegiance into *the* organization that represents, defends, protects and cares for *all* Palestinians.[6] The PLO serves the short- and long-term needs of Palestinians and, above all, represents their political will and national aspirations. It has become for them the organization which embodies the dream of the long-awaited homeland, Palestine.

For Palestinians living in the West Bank, Gaza and Israel, the PLO symbolizes the end of occupation. The PLO represents to them liberation, freedom, sovereignty and national dignity. It has become in the Palestinian consciousness the state, the government, the homeland and the refuge for the Palestinian people. Some have even used the term "PLO" interchangeably with "the Palestinian people."

THE PLO—A GOVERNMENT IN EXILE

The PLO could not have achieved this status had its institutional and constitutional structures been formed in a manner other than that which its founding fathers had chosen. Additionally, in the process of the development of the PLO, many important changes have occurred which warrant discussion.

The PLO has a state structure similar to other established nations and systems of government. The following are its three main components:

1. *Palestine National Council* The Palestine National Council (PNC) constitutes the PLO's legislative branch and includes the Central Council of the PNC. Whereas the founding fathers conceived of and created the PNC in the Palestine National Charter, the Central Council was introduced in the early 1970s and incorporated in the PLO by a decision of the PNC.

2. *Executive Committee* The Executive Committee serves as the PLO's executive branch of government. It is responsible for day-to-day operations of the PLO and its members head offices of various departments similar to ministers in the cabinets of other state governments.

3. *Judiciary* The judicial branch of government of the PLO has not yet been fully developed or formed into a structure like those existing within other nations. This in large part is due to the fact that Palestinians live within territory occupied by Israel, or in diaspora. Palestinians do not have as yet a state of their own and, therefore, are subject to the civil and commercial rule of law and jurisdiction of host or occupation governments. However, in constitutional matters concerning the PLO and specific other areas, the PNC executive committee and other bodies of the PNC serve in the capacity of a

judicial body. They separately and collectively can suggest amend-ments to the Palestine National Charter, as well as review internal PLO disputes with final judicial rule. This is discussed more fully in later pages.

Before analyzing the structure of the PLO, it is necessary to ex-plain the political principles which have guided the Palestinian leadership and people ever since the establishment of the organiza-tion in 1964.

At their first meeting of the PNC the founding fathers adopted two major documents: the Palestine National Charter and the Basic Law of the PLO. Some writers have rightly described the first to be the "Declaration of Independence" of the Palestinian people and the second to be the "Constitution" of the Palestinian state.[7] The principles enshrined in the Charter and the Basic Law have guided the PLO ever since. The democratic significance of these principles is demonstrated in the fact that changing, annulling, or amending any part of them requires a majority of two thirds of the members of the PNC.[8]

The Charter and the Basic Law adopted by the founding fathers in May 1964 underwent major changes during the fourth session of the PNC held in Cairo in July 1968. Whereas the Charter of 1964 had 24 articles, that of 1968 had 33 articles. Of the 24 articles in the Charter of 1964, 15 articles were amended, 11 articles were left unchanged, two articles were annulled and seven new ones were passed and added to the Charter.[9]

Articles in the Basic Law were also amended, the most important of which were the separation of powers between the legislative and executive branches of the PLO and the stipulation that the PNC elects the Executive Committee of the PLO, which in turn elects its Chair-man. The Basic Law of 1964 gave the PNC the right to elect only the Chairman of the Executive Committee who then chose its members.

From reviewing the historical development of the PLO, one can conclude that the four PNC sessions of paramount importance to its structural development were:

1. The first PNC meeting in 1964.

2. The fourth PNC meeting in July 1968 which established fun-damental structural changes in the PLO. This meeting reflected the

increased influence of the Fedayeen organizations on the Palestinian, Arab and international levels.

3. The fifth PNC meeting held in February 1969 in Cairo, during which the Fedayeen organizations officially formed the Executive Committee of the PLO. During this meeting, Yasser Arafat was elected Chairman of the Executive Committee of the PLO, a position which he holds to this day.

4. The 17th session of the PNC was held in November 1964, in Amman. This session is very important from the political and structural perspectives. It reflected the sovereign will of the Palestinian people to independently determine their decision-making process, which affected the PLO as an organization and the future of the Palestinian people.

The 17th session must be seen in light of the political and military maneuvering by major regional and international powers to prevent its convening. At the time, serious attempts were made to block the session, which for the PNC's protagonists, would result in the elimination of the PLO as a viable political organization, representative of the Palestinian people. The 17th session is a cornerstone in PLO development for reasons detailed in this study, and from its results are based these analyses.

The PLO—a Democratic System

Among the principles originally laid down by the Charter and the Basic Law is the emphasis on democracy, a multi-party system, pluralism, secularism, the art of political persuasion, consensus and collective leadership.

Article Three of the Basic Law defined these principles in the following manner:

"Relations within the Organization [PLO] shall be based on commitment to national struggle and action, and on a close link among the different levels of the organization, from its base upward to its collective leadership, on the basis of the following principles: the minority shall defer to the will of the majority, public confidence must be achieved through persuasion and consensus, the movement of the Palestinian struggle shall be continued, support for the armed Palestinian revolution, and every possible effort shall be made to ensure that it continues and escalates so that the impetus of the masses toward liberation may take its course until victory is achieved."

The PLO's political process is founded on two pillars: a pluralistic, multi-party system and collective leadership. There is within the PLO a dominant ruling party, the Palestine National Liberation Movement ("Al Fateh" or "Fateh"), which, in consultation with other organizations and politically active members of the Palestinian community, decides to a large extent the political guidelines to be followed by the PLO. There is also the "loyal opposition" which is seated in the Council and forms an active minority.

It must be noted that there are no major differences between the ruling party and its opposition on matters of political principles governing the formulation of guidelines and general strategies of the PLO. There are, however, major differences on specific matters of tactics and implementation of adopted policies. These differences are occasionally severe enough to prompt the opposition parties to suspend their membership or to refuse participation in forming the Executive Committee. Additionally, there is an extra-parliamentary opposition composed of extremist elements, whose objectives are hidden behind radical, nationalist terminology. This extra-parliamentary opposition is not officially recognized by the PLO and constitutes the fringe groups which were responsible for the fall 1983 inter-Palestinian conflict in Lebanon. They are without question extremist and against the democratically elected and legitimate leadership of the PLO.

Although Fateh is by far the largest and most powerful party among the various Palestinian organizations which comprise the PLO—and could at any time easily form and control the Executive Committee—it has, since 1969, opted for the formation of a coalition form of government.

Fateh, because it is the largest group within the PLO, has assigned itself three of the 15 portfolios of the Executive Committee. These portfolios are the chairmanship of the Executive Committee, the Political Department and the Department of National Relations. Al Fateh, however, does not endeavor to dominate the PLO.

When Ahmad Shuqayri, the first chairman of the Executive Committee, came under pressure to resign in 1967, he offered Fateh the PLO leadership. Fateh, however, rejected his proposal and insisted on continued wide political participation in the PLO. Fateh leaders understand the PLO to be a united national front for all Palestinian activists, that is, the political and military organizations, the mass organizations and the independents.[10]

By adopting this position, Fateh maintains harmony with the democratic mandates of the PLO Charter: that the PLO is a united front among the forces of the Palestinian revolution. Article 26 of the Charter defines the PLO as follows:

"The Palestine Liberation Organization, the representative of the Palestine revolutionary forces, is responsible for the Palestinian Arab people's struggle to regain and liberate their homeland, to return to it and to exercise the right of self-determination in it. This responsibility extends to all political, military and financial aspects and to all that concerns the question of Palestine on the inter-Arab and international levels."

Pressures on Fateh to dominate the PLO and the Palestine national movement have not only come from Palestinian sources. Equal pressures have been exerted on Fateh by various Arab governments to proclaim itself to be representative of all the PLO. At the 1969 Arab League summit, Arab heads of state proposed immediate recognition of Fateh itself as the Palestine Liberation Organization. To his credit, Chairman Arafat rejected this proposal and insisted on the united front character of the PLO. Once more, Fateh reaffirmed adherence to the principles of unity regarding the effective political participation of all the forces of the Palestine revolution. A foundation based upon the interests of the Palestinian people placed above narrow political party considerations has been and continues to be Fateh's primary internal structural objective.

For Fateh, the issue is a matter of principle and of prime importance to the process of Palestinian political education and participation, not only for members of Fateh, but for the other PLO parties — its partners on the road to national liberation.

Since Fateh has opted from the very beginning for the united front concept as a basis for the PLO's political organization, it was only natural to extend this principle to the function of the bodies and organs within the PLO, as in the nomination of members of the Executive Committee or in the elections of its popular organizations.

The record shows that without Fateh's strict adherence to the principles of coalition government at all levels, other PLO organizations would have been unable to win any elections or to have their candidates elected in the various organs of the PLO on the basis of one-man, one-vote. Candidates from non-Fateh parties have been consistently elected because of Fateh's coalition-building efforts within the PLO.[11]

INSTITUTIONS OF THE PALESTINE LIBERATION ORGANIZATION

Having discussed how the formative years of the PLO helped shaped the composition of its infrastructure, as well as Fateh's role in insuring a multi-dimensional leadership and adherence to democratic principles, it is instructive to analyze in detail the PLO's institutions.

THE PALESTINE NATIONAL COUNCIL

Article 7A of the Basic Law[12] stipulates that the Palestine National Council (the Palestinian parliament-in-exile) is the democratically elected, supreme authority of the PLO and represents the Palestinian people, both inside and outside occupied Palestine. Consequently, it includes in its membership representatives of the Palestinian people from all walks of life. The Basic Law stipulates in Article 5 that members of the PNC are to be elected by the Palestinian people, through direct ballot according to electoral laws drawn up by the Executive Committee of the PLO.

The term of each PNC is three years. It convenes annually upon the invitation or request of its chairman. The chairman can call the PNC into an extraordinary or special session upon the request of the Executive Committee or of one-quarter of its members. If the chairman himself does not convene a PNC session, the PNC is considered to be in session at the time and place requested by its members or by the Executive Committee.

Taking into consideration the uniqueness of the Palestinian situation and in order to meet the demands of the national liberation struggle, the principle of proportional representation within the PNC has been adopted as a practical measure. This principle is based on geographic, political and functional considerations, and insures the representation of Palestinian communities in diaspora, as well as providing the participation of various political groups active in the Palestinian national movement.

Thus, PNC membership includes a number of categories that do not have equivalents in legislative systems established in their own territory. These are referred to as:

1. the political-military organizations (hereafter referred to as the "Organizations");

2. the Mass Organizations;

3. representatives of the Palestinian communities, including refugee camps and bedouin tribes, and well-known personalities in Palestinian communities, known as the "Independent Personalities"; and

4. the Palestine National Liberation Army.

For all practical purposes these groups fulfill the role of political parties in other democratic political systems. For example, the Mass Organizations are equivalent to trade unions and other labor organizations. Refugee camps, however, represent a unique characteristic of the Palestinian situation in diaspora. Total PNC membership as of the 17th session is officially 430 members. The total now stands at 426, due to the death of four members since 1984. Distribution of PNC membership at its 17th session was as follows:

1. *Organizations*

Fateh	33
PFLP	12
DFLP	10
SAIQA	12
Arab Liberation Front	8
Other Organizations	8
TOTAL	83

The 83 organization members represent 19.3 percent of PNC membership.

2. *The Mass Organizations* The 112 Mass- Organization (trade union) members represent 26 percent of PNC membership.

3. *Communities and Independents* Palestinian representatives from Arab countries and other parts of the world, mainly North and South America, form the bulk of the Communities and Independents membership in the PNC, at present 191 members or 44 percent of PNC membership. This can be broken down into two categories:

A. Refugee camps, the Bedouin tribes and major Palestinian communities have representatives from Egypt (5), the GCC states (24), Jordan (27), Lebanon (12), Saudi Arabia (6), and Syria (9), for a total of 83, or 19.3 percent of PNC membership.

B. Other independent representatives total 108, including 11 representatives from South America and 9 representatives from North America, or 25.1 percent of PNC membership.

4. *The Palestine National Liberation Army* The 44 Palestine National Liberation Army members represent 10.2 percent of PNC membership.

In addition to the membership above, 188 seats of the PNC are reserved for Palestinian representatives from the occupied territories of the West Bank and the Gaza Strip. This number, however, is not counted in the quorum of the PNC. In this category are the heads of the municipal councils, mayors and leaders of trade unions which have, whenever possible, been directly elected by the Palestinians living under Israeli occupation. For example, when the Israeli authorities in 1980 deported the mayors of Hebron and Halhoul, the late Fahd Al- Qawasmeh and Muhammad Melhem, both men were able to take up their seats in the PNC as representatives of their respective constituencies.

On the other hand, while there are no seats reserved for the Palestinian population of the territories occupied in 1948 (in Israel), Palestinian community leaders or activists who were deported by Israel from these territories are seated in the PNC. A few of these are the Palestinian poet Mahmoud Darwish, the political and human rights activists Sabri Jiryes and Imad Shaqqur, and Habib Qahwaji, a founding member of the "Al Ard" movement ("The Land" movement) in the early 1960s.

Election of PNC representatives is a function of the particular Palestinian situation. Some representatives are directly elected, whenever direct elections are possible, according to the principle of one-man, one-vote. This has been the case in Lebanon, Kuwait and

North and South America. Others are directly elected by their own "constituencies," i.e., by their own organizations to whom they are directly responsible, such as the political-military Organizations and the Mass Organizations. The PLO's founding fathers decided that, since these representatives are directly elected by the members of their organizations and because there is proportional representation governing these categories, these organizations simply designate their own delegates to the PNC.

Independents are chosen on the basis of their contribution to the Palestinian cause whether professional, social, economic, or cultural. Again, due to the complexity of the Palestinian situation, the election of independent candidates is complicated. Whenever possible, the independent representatives are elected directly, as in Lebanon, Kuwait and Latin America. Where direct elections are not possible, a special committee is elected by the PNC to consult the various worldwide Palestinian constituencies to nominate respected Palestinians who share the general trend of public opinion in these constituencies. This committee then submits its comprehensive report to the PNC where the names are discussed and voted upon. Those independent candidates with a majority vote of the committee become members of the PNC representing their respective constituencies.

Finally, the representatives to the PNC from the Palestine National Liberation Army are officially designated by their commander-in-chief, who also holds the position of the PLO's Executive Committee Chairman. This designation process, however, is conducted in consultation with the other members of the Executive Committee and the chairman of the PNC, thus assuring representation of the Army in the PNC by consensus.

The PNC is run by a secretariat entitled the Office of the Presidency of the PNC. The elected chairman of the PNC is assisted by two elected vice-chairmen and a secretary. All four are members of the PNC. The chairman, vice-chairmen and secretary are elected during the PNC plenary sessions. The Basic Law stipulates that only the chairman assumes his position on a full-time basis.

There are two types of committees of the PNC: discussion committees and standing committees, which are described as follows:

The Discussion Committees

Because the PNC meets once a year, it has developed its own procedure, as stipulated in the Basic Law, for discussing issues and adopting decisions and resolutions.

Members of the PNC join or are appointed to committees established at PNC opening sessions following approval of the session's agenda. After the presentation of reports by the Executive Committee and the Palestine National Fund, a general debate is opened in the plenary session. At the close of this general debate, the committees go in session to discuss, debate and submit recommendations on issues placed before them. When the committees complete their deliberations, the recommendations they adopt are sent to the plenary session of the PNC for further discussion, amendment, or approval. Once these recommendations are approved and voted upon they become decisions or resolutions of the PNC. In accordance with the practice of the PNC, certain topics of discussion have become established on the agenda in every recent session. As a result, the committees which deal with these topics have become established committees.

Up to and including the 17th session, the PNC had the following permanent discussion committees as stipulated in the Basic Law:

Political Committee
Financial Committee
Occupied Homeland Committee
Mass Organizations Committee
Military Committee
Information and Culture Committee
Education and Higher Education Committee
Palestinian Affairs in Lebanon Committee
Judicial Committee

These committees last for the duration of the session of the PNC. The only committee which has not been permanent was the Political Committee, also known as the Foreign Affairs Committee.

The Standing Committees

A serious shortcoming existed prior to the establishment of PNC standing committees. Specifically, issues which required follow up,

discussion or decision-making by the members of the PNC, when
in recess, were left open to be handled outside the institutional
framework of the PNC, either by establishing ad-hoc committees,
or by referring the issues to the Presidium of the PNC or to the relevant departments of the PLO.

In order to rectify this shortcoming, the 17th session of the PNC
decided to establish the following eight specialized standing committees in the PNC, as follows:

   The Judiciary Committee
   The Parliamentary and Foreign Affairs Committee
   The Committee for the Affairs of the Occupied Homeland
   Information, Culture, Education and Learning Committee
   The Arab-European Dialogue Committee
   The Administrative Reform Committee
   The Disciplinary and Control Committee The Investigative
      Committee

The decision also stipulated that the PNC can establish any other
committee it deems necessary.

Standing committees have the same life span as the PNC, and
membership on each does not exceed 10 representatives. The function of these committees has been limited to the study of issues referred to them by the Secretariat or the Executive Committee, extending advice and recommendations to the Secretariat or Executive
Committee whenever requested, and any other matter referred to
the attention of the committee. Each committee chooses its chairman and rapporteur from among its members. While discussion committee membership is open and unlimited to all PNC members,
standing committees are limited to 10. The eight committees,
therefore, have a total number of 80 members.

Loss of Membership

A number of conditions govern the loss or suspension of PNC
membership. Among these, as defined in Article 73 of the By-laws
of the PNC, are as follows:
   —absence without permission of, or without providing acceptable
excuses to, the PNC during three consecutive sessions;
   —working for a government or institution of a non-Arab state

which creates certain doubts on the representative's stand; and

— undertaking an action which is in contradiction to the PLO Charter or its Basic Law.

Furthermore, Article 78 stipulates that membership in the PNC is lost as a result of death or resignation. Another form of losing membership in the PNC, which is not stipulated clearly in the PNC Charter, results from reapportionment based on the principle of proportional representation in the PNC as applied to the distribution of seats among the politico-military Organizations and the Mass Organizations. In this category of proportional representation a block of seats is allocated to every organization, leaving it the responsibility of each to decide changes in delegates among its representatives to the PNC.

Similarly, if a given organization wants to replace one or more of its delegates, it can do so by handing the Presidium of the PNC a written memorandum signed by the leadership of the particular organization indicating the names to be dropped and added. The memorandum must be received by the Presidium before the opening session of the PNC. Change of membership usually results from internal elections within specific organizations. Neither the Presidium nor the Council has the power to vote against such a move. It is to be noted that since 1964, Article 73 has only been invoked once; during the 17th session held in Amman.

Article 74 of Chapter 8, which regulates the composition of the PNC, stipulates that one fifth of total PNC membership must submit a written, signed memorandum to suspend or drop membership of any members. Officially, the member in question must be informed of such a request against him, and the request must be put before the PNC in its opening session when members' credentials are voted upon.

Articles 75, 76 and 77 stipulate further safeguards for the protection of membership, among which is the formation of an ad hoc committee to look into any accusation put forward against a member. Such committees must report their findings to the PNC within 48 hours. The PNC then devotes one special session to this particular case. The member concerned has the right to attend this session and participate in its discussions, but has no voting rights when the measure is acted upon, and must be absent during the voting procedure.

This complicated procedure reflects the concern and high value the Palestinian people place on safeguarding PNC membership, protecting their democratic rights and freedom of expression, and their political awareness and maturity in protecting their political processes and institutions from the whims of dictatorial or authoritarian rule.

As mentioned above, Article 73 was invoked in 1984 against six members of the PNC accused of instigating a military coup within the PLO and leading military attacks against the PLO leadership and the Palestinian refugee camps in Tripoli, Lebanon, in late 1983. The six were Ahmed Jibril, Fadel Shroro, Khaled Abdel Majid, Elias Shoufani, Sameer Ghosheh and Sameeh Abu Kweik. However, because immunity of PNC members is a sacred right, and due to the above-mentioned provisions in Article 74, 75, 76 and 77, the PNC did not make a final decision on their dismissal. In accordance with these articles, the PNC Judiciary Committee recommended that their membership be suspended until the stipulations of the above mentioned articles be carried out by the Chairman of the PNC. The matter was referred to the next PNC session for a final decision.

Other PNC members representing particular organizations, e.g., Fateh, and who participated in the late 1983 anti-PLO military campaign in Lebanon were replaced by their own organizations. Most notable were the cases of Abu Musa and Abu Khaled al Amleh, the two most senior leaders of the attempted coup.

THE CENTRAL COUNCIL

In 1964, when the PLO founding fathers deliberated the PLO's Charter and Basic Law, they did not envision the formation of a second house within the PLO's legislative branch, and instead chose a unicameral legislature. In this respect, they were influenced by then-existing and past republican Arab states with one-house legislatures.

However, parliaments in other states are normally established on their own territory and within their own governments, and are therefore capable of scheduling legislative sessions throughout the year. These meetings are usually attended by all elected members without significant administrative or financial complications. Furthermore, it is the norm in most republican states that members are elected on a full-time basis to represent their constituencies and carry out legislative responsibilities.

The Palestinian people, however, lack both territory and the state apparatus enjoyed by most peoples, and are dispersed throughout the four corners of the globe. As a result, when the PNC is convened its members arrive from points all over the world and, since they normally have other full-time professions, they do not receive salaries as PNC representatives.

It is therefore quite difficult to convene the PNC in the same manner as other parliaments due to logistic difficulties, financial expenses, accommodations and the necessary absence of members from their businesses and occupations. Because of these hardships, it was decided to convene the PNC only once a year.

However, the PLO's success in maintaining the Palestinian cause and increasing the organization's relations with the outside world paradoxically created a number of problems. Because of the PLO's institutionalization and broader outreach, the PNC itself was not capable of handling important questions on a regular basis. Decisions had to be made more frequently and at a higher level on problems of a legislative or quasi-legislative nature. To remedy the situation, it was decided to establish a second but smaller legislative body which would function as a link between the PNC when it was in recess and the PLO's Executive Committee.

In its 11th session held in Cairo in 1973, the PNC established a Central Council from its own membership to follow up on its recommendations and to participate in the implementation of its resolutions. The Central Council initially was created with 21 members, it was headed by the Chairman of the PNC, and the membership was distributed among the various Palestinian movement political power centers represented in the PNC at the time as follows:

Fateh	4
Saiga	2
PFLP	2
DFLP	2
The Arab Liberation Front	2
Mass Organizations (Unions)	6
Independents	5

The Council was assigned consultative functions to the PLO leadership and its recommendations cannot contradict either the Charter or previous PNC resolutions. During the 17th session of the PNC, a special resolution was passed on the Central Council defining its composition, membership and function. Article I of this resolution stipulates that the Council is formed from among the membership of the PNC. The Central Council's terms have the same duration as the time between two normal sessions of the PNC, and it is headed by the Chairman of the PNC.

Central Council membership, according to Article II of the resolution, includes:

1. the Chairman and all members of the Executive Committee of the PLO;

2. the Chairman and the members of the PNC Secretariat;

3. the presidents or the secretaries-generals of the mass organizations, unions, syndicates, or their respective representatives in the PNC;

4. representatives of organizations which are not accredited in the PNC. (This stipulation is important because there are organizations which are not accredited in the PNC as separate entities, but which have members in the PNC elected in their personal capacity.);

5. three representatives from the Military Council who are designated by the commander-in-chief; and

6. twenty five members representing the PNC's independents.

Whereas the Central Council's membership originally totalled 21 in 1973, its membership now is 72, distributed as follows:

1. the Executive Committee of the PLO, which usually has 15 members and has now only 11;

2. the Secretariat of the PNC, with four members;

3. the independents with 25 members. (These were designated, as an exception, by the Executive Committee of the PLO in coordination with the PNC's Secretariat. The resolution on the creation of the Central Council stipulates, as mentioned above, that under normal circumstances these 25 members should be elected directly at the PNC session. The independents also include representatives of Palestinian communities abroad.); and

4. the Organizations membership distributed as follows: with the exception of Fateh, which has six members, four other organizations accredited to the PNC have two representatives each. Together they have 14 representatives.

The original 1973 resolution establishing the Central Council stipulated consultative functions for this body. However, a resolution at the 1984 PNC session expanded these functions to include the following functions:

1. making necessary decisions on issues and questions referred by the Executive Committee within the framework of PNC resolutions;

2. discussing and adopting plans put before the Central Council by the Executive Committee;

3. insuring that the Executive Committee implements resolutions adopted by the PNC; and

4. overseeing the activities of the different departments of the PLO and submitting any relevant recommendations to the Executive Committee.

The Central Council, therefore, has more than a purely consultative role. First, it has a legislative function in the sense that it can make recommendations on enacting new laws. Second, it has an executive role, whereby it can adopt resolutions and make decisions concerning the implementation of certain policies or programs delayed by the Executive Committee. Third, it also has a political role to play in the sense that the political communique issued at the conclusion of its meetings has a moral force which neither the executive branch nor the legislative branch can ignore. Finally, it oversees the activities and programs of all the various PLO departments.

THE EXECUTIVE BRANCH

1. The Executive Committee

The Charter and Basic Law stipulate clearly that there should be a separation of powers between the legislative and the executive branches of the PLO.[13] This, however, was not always the case, especially during the first three years of the PLO's existence, from 1964 to 1967, when Ahmad Shuqayri held both the position of chairman of the Executive Committee and speaker of the Palestine National Council. Furthermore, Shuqayri vested himself with presidential powers which, during the formative years of the PLO's development, few within the organization were ready to challenge. This is in large part due to the founding fathers seeing the establishment of the PLO itself as a very unique and positive step forward in the interests of the Palestinian people — the first time in two decades that the Arab states sanctioned the establishment of an independent Palestinian body.

The representatives of the Palestinian people to the first PNC meeting held in Jerusalem in late May 1964, and who were to a great extent selected by Shuqayri himself, in consultation with the dominant Palestinian social forces, accepted the establishment of the PLO with all the flaws that mark the formative years of any political grouping. The PLO, however, faced a great deal of criticism from the Organizations, particularly from Fateh, which did not participate officially in this first PNC meeting.

Articles 13 and 15 of the Basic Law stipulate that the PNC selects the Executive Committee (i.e., the PLO's cabinet) from its own members. The Committee itself selects its own chairman. The Committee is in permanent session and its members work on a full-time basis. The Committee and its members are responsible to the PNC individually and collectively for the execution and implementation of the policies, plans and programs drawn up and adopted by the PNC.

Article 14 of the Basic Law sets the membership of the Executive Committee at a maximum of 15 members, including the Chairman and the head of the Board of Directors of the Palestine National Fund (PNF). The latter in particular is elected to the Executive Committee in this capacity. The Executive Committee functions, for all practical purposes and by law, as the cabinet in any other country with a modern parliamentary system.

In its first meeting after being elected, the Executive Committee chooses among its members the heads (ministers) of departments, and announces these selections in an official public communique. Each officer then receives his portfolio or department, as defined in Article 18 of the Basic Law. Each department has its own bureaucracy. One source has estimated the total personnel of the various PLO departments at 5,000.[14]

Since 1964 these departments have been redefined, renamed and expanded. Based on elections held at the 17th session in Amman, the members of the Executive Committee of the PLO are as follows: Yasser Arafat, Chairman of the Executive Committee and Head of the Military Department; Farouq Qaddoumi, Head of the Political Department (or ministry of foreign affairs); Mahmoud Abbas, Head of the Department of National Relations; Jamal Sourani, Secretary of the Executive Committee and Head of the Department of Administrative Affairs; Ahmad Abd Al-Rahim, Head of the Department of Mass Organizations and Head of the Social and Labor Department; Archbishop Elia Khoury, Executive Committee member without portfolio; Jaweed Al Ghussein, Head of the Board of Directors of the Palestine National Fund; Fahd al Qawasmeh, Head of the Occupied Homeland Department (Qawasmeh was assassinated at the end of December 1984, one month after his election, and was replaced by Mohammed Melhem); Muhammad Melhem, Head of the Higher Learning and Education Department; and Muhammad Abbas, Head of the Department for Refugees.

At the 17th session, the PNC decided for reasons of national unity to leave several seats on the Executive Committee for independent members and representatives of organizations which did not or were unable to attend that session. This explains why only 11 members were elected to the Executive Committee, with the remaining four portfolios reserved for those not in attendance. The departments affected by these vacancies are the Department of Information and the Department of National Guidance.

These departments are now temporarily headed by elected members of the Executive Committee who serve these responsibilities in addition to their own departments. The daily operations of each of these departments are usually managed by an assigned director general.

There are other departments, councils, centers and agencies which fall within the jurisdiction of the Executive Committee, but whose heads do not have portfolios in the Committee. Examples of these are the Planning Department and the PLO Research Center, which are run by a director general even though Article 18 of the Basic Law stipulates "the establishment of a research department and specialized institutions." There is also the Council on Higher Education, Culture and Science, which is headed by Dr. Ahmad Sidqi Al-Dajani, a veteran former senior PLO Executive Committee member, who also serves as Chairman of the PNC's Arab-European Dialogue Committee.

According to Article 15 of the Basic Law, the Executive Committee is the 'supreme executive authority of the PLO,' which is endowed in Article 16 with the following four major functions:

1. to represent the Palestinian people;

2. to regulate and supervise the various bodies and institutions of the PLO;

3. to issue directives, draw programs and adopt decisions regarding the activities of the PLO in conformity with the Charter and the Basic Law of the PLO; and

4. to carry out the PLO's financial policies and prepare its budget.

It should be noted that neither the PLO's Charter nor the Basic Law make any reference to the role of a president or a prime minister representing the Palestinian people. These two functions are the prerogative of the Chairman of the Executive Committee. It was the mark left on PLO politics by Chairman Arafat's charismatic personality and his style of leadership, which allowed him to assume this dual function. Thus, Yasser Arafat serves not only as Chairman of the Executive Committee, (i.e., the equivalent of prime minister in other governments) but has also evolved into the "president" of the PLO, and the symbol of the Palestinian people and their national aspirations.

This role contrasts with that played by Ahmad Shuqayri, who led the Palestinian people by virtue of combining the positions of both the presidency of the PNC and the chairmanship of the Executive Committee. Yasser Arafat's charismatic personality, style of leadership and his art of persuasion and motivation have enabled him to successfully combine these two functions into one. As a result, Chairman Arafat has frequently been officially received and accredited the status of head of state when visiting foreign countries. He has also been received as a prime minister of a democratically elected parliamentary system.

Similar to the cabinets of other governments, the Executive Committee assumes the state and policy responsibilities of the PLO in accordance with general resolutions drawn and adopted by the PNC. Since the Executive Committee is elected by and responsible to the PNC, it submits its resignation to the PNC at the end of every ordinary session, i.e., every three years. The PNC is empowered to reelect the Committee or completely change or reshuffle its membership. As long as the Committee enjoys the confidence of the PNC it remains in office. Generally speaking, the distribution of power within the Executive Committee reflects the distribution of power within the PNC itself.

At its meetings, two-thirds of the Executive Committee membership constitutes a quorum. During the last session of the PNC it was decided that an Executive Committee quorum is based on 11 total members and not 15, due to the four vacant positions mentioned previously. Decisions are taken by simple majority of the Executive Committee members present.

In its history, the functions of the Executive Committee have never been interrupted except once, when it was dismantled by its first Chairman, Ahmad Shuqayri. In December 1966, Shuqayri replaced the Executive Committee with a "revolutionary council" to assume the responsibility of preparing the Palestinians for a war of liberation. At the time, Shuqayri even withheld the names of the Council members and their activities because, as he claimed, some of them lived in Jordan.[15]

However, rapid developments in the Middle East and the June 1967 Israeli war of aggression cancelled Shuqayri's plans. He was forced to resign on December 24, 1967, under widespread pressure from the Palestinian people and the leadership of Fateh, the largest and most powerful of the PLO's Organizations. Except for this brief period, the Executive Committee has functioned without interruption since its inception.

The adherence of the Palestinian people to democratic process, and to consultation and deliberation prior to decision- making, led to the establishment of two additional bodies outside the framework of the PLO's Basic Law. The two organs have served as a means to arrive at decisions on resolutions of important political nature and which warrant consensus among all the organizations and independent representatives. Their creation was a function of the distinctive nature of the conditions of Palestinian existence. The two innovations are the Council of the Secretaries-General and its successor, the Council of the Palestinian Leadership, as discussed below:

The Council of the Secretaries-General

In the seventies, when Lebanon became the major base for the Palestinian revolution, the PLO's leadership and its Executive Committee concluded that it was in the interests of the Palestinian people to include the secretaries-general of the various PLO organizations in their meetings to facilitate unanimous decision-making. In essence, this was done because several secretaries-general did not personally assume the portfolios allocated to their organizations by the Executive Committee, and instead opted to delegate such authority to a deputy within the organization.

In order to have the direct and formal participation of these secretaries-general in the PLO's decision-making process, the Council of the Secretaries-General was institutionalized to convene at regular intervals in order for them to discuss and determine specific questions. The Council included in its meetings various organizations' secretaries-general, the members of the Executive Committee and the chairman of the PNC.

The Council of the Palestinian Leadership

Following the departure of the PLO from Beirut, the Council of the Secretaries-General ceased to exist in the form developed prior to 1982. It was replaced by the Council of the Palestinian Leadership, which differentiated itself from Central Council meetings only by emphasis since its membership is more broadly based. Its membership usually includes the entire membership of the Central Council plus all or most of the members of the Central Committee of Fateh, who are generally more able to attend its meetings. It is to be noted that representatives of other PLO organizations frequently participate, as well.

The Council of Palestinian Leadership and the PNC's Central Council both serve a consultative function and have a moral power based upon their wide representation of the Palestinian people. Following their convention, their recommendations are automatically submitted to the Executive Committee for consideration, which in turn review adoption of new policies for the PLO.

Having reviewed the leadership structure of the PLO's executive branch—the Executive Committee—it is useful at this juncture to examine the various departments under the Executive Committee's jurisdiction. These departments, by and large, fulfill the social, economic, political and security needs of the Palestinian people in absence of an established state system within a society based on territory.

2. The Palestine National Fund

Throughout much of 1985 and 1986, a concerted disinformation campaign was waged in various international mass media concerning the finances of the PLO and its alleged billions of dollars safely deposited in West European banks.[16] Despite the Arabic proverb that "a reputation of wealth is better than a reputation of poverty," the PLO's actual wealth is far from that imagined in Western public opinion.

The individuals and institutions behind the disinformation campaign had ulterior motives, among which was the discrediting of the PLO among Palestinian, Arab and international public opinion. The campaign also sought to tarnish the image of the Chairman of the Executive Committee by insinuating that the PLO had secret funds which were withheld from the Palestinian people and allowed its leadership to live lavishly. The campaign ultimately sought to place the PLO's leadership in a defensive position and force them to reveal financial and budgetary matters allegedly held in secrecy.

This disinformation campaign failed to achieve its objectives because the PLO has neither secret accounts in Western banks nor are its income and budget a secret—the budget of the PLO is presented openly at each PNC session. It is discussed and debated openly and after its adoption, the PLO's budget is published for public distribution. In fact, the PNC's entire proceedings are published, including deliberations over the PLO's budget, and given as wide as possible distribution to the Palestinian, Arab and international media.

The question of both financing the PLO and establishing the Palestine National Fund (PNF) were a significant priority in the minds of the PLO's founding fathers when drafting the Charter and Basic Law. These issues have drawn heated debate during every session of the PNC. The importance of day-to-day financing of the PLO and establishing an endowment for future Palestinian generations is reflected in the fact that the head of the PNF's Board of Directors is elected to the Executive Committee of the PLO.

The first PNC resolved, in accordance with Article 24 of the Basic Law, to establish the PNF to finance the activities of the PLO. The PNC also decided, in accordance with a special law governing the PNF, to establish a Board of Directors to manage the PNF's affairs. Sources of revenue for the PNF are stipulated in Article 25 of the Basic Law as follows:

1. a fixed tax levied on the Palestinians, to be collected according to special regulations drawn up for that purpose;

2. financial assistance from Arab governments;

3. a postal "stamp of liberation" issued by the postal departments of Arab states;

4. contributions and endowments;

5. loans and contributions from Arab governments or other friendly nations; and

6. any additional sources approved by the PNC.

The process of collecting taxes and contributions is both extremely complex and understandably difficult, and is one of the most serious responsibilities of the PLO. Concerning taxes levied from Palestinians, it is understood that most of the Palestinians concerned reside in Arab countries where by mutual agreement between the PLO and host government guarantees are made for the orderly collection of receipts. More often than not, however, this process is hampered by the host Arab governments and is dependent on the condition of relations existing between the PLO and the given Arab government.

For example, the PNC financial report presented at the 17th session in 1984 stated: "Taxes levied in Libya during the past two years have not yet reached the PNF. Contacts have been established with Libyan officials regarding this issue, however these efforts have been of no avail."[17] It further stated: "It is necessary to point out the decline in taxes recently levied in the Gulf states due to the difficult economic situation in the Gulf and the reflection of this situation on our people working there."[18]

The PNC financial report accused Libya of "confiscating the revenues of the PNF which have been levied from the Palestinians working in Libya and contributing these funds to what it calls the Palestinian General Peoples' Conference," i.e., the revolutionary committees which work against the Palestinian Revolution.[19] It further stated "the equivalent of one month's salary had been deducted from all Arab and Palestinian workers in Libya during the siege of Beirut and donated to the Palestinian Revolution. These funds have never been received by the PNF. They were used for political and military purposes by Libya against the Palestinian Revolution."

A second point regarding financial contributions from the Arab governments is also a point of contention between the PLO and the Arab states. While several Arab states such as Saudi Arabia have made their contributions to the PLO on a regular basis and on schedule, the performance of others leaves much to be desired.

The 1978 Arab Summit conference in Baghdad decided that the wealthy Arab states should support the PLO with an annual $300 million contribution for ten consecutive years, beginning in 1979. It was resolved that each state pay the amount assigned to it in three equal allotments according to the following schedule[20]:

Country	Total ($M)	Each Annual Allotment ($M)
United Arab Emirates	34.4	11.4
Algeria	21.4	7.1
Iraq	44.6	4.9
Saudi Arabia	85.7	28.6
Qatar	19.8	6.6
Kuwait	47.1	15.7
Libya	47.1	15.7
TOTAL	300.0	100.0

In its report to the 17th PNC session, the PNF complained that these shares were neither paid in full nor received at all for the fiscal year 1983-1984.[21] The report continued: "... as for years 1983 and 1984, the PNF received only one share from Kuwait in 1983 and part of its first share for 1984. Until now, we have not received the rest of the shares for 1983 and 1984. The United Arab Emirates has paid only one share for 1984. Qatar has paid one share for the year 1983 and a part of its first share for the year 1984, but did not pay any of its dues for 1983 and 1984. The Kingdom of Saudi Arabia, however, paid all its commitments for 1983 and 1984. As to the other

Arab states, they have not fulfilled their pledges for these two years."[22]

These examples demonstrate the extent to which the PLO is dependent on the goodwill and cooperation of the Arab governments. Furthermore, it demonstrates the difficulties and obstacles involved in conducting sound financial policies free of political constraints. It is still hoped that the Arab states will cooperate closer with the PLO in the future and help alleviate the burden shouldered by the Palestinian people, whether under Israeli occupation or in diaspora.

The PNF is governed by a board of directors whose chairman is elected by the PNC. As previously mentioned, the PNF chairman automatically becomes a member of the Executive Committee of the PLO. The other ten members of the PNF's Board of directors are elected by the Executive Committee and hold a three-year term, as does the PNF chairman. The Board assigns a director general to the PNF who assembles a responsible staff to conduct its duties. The Board's regular meetings are attended by the Chairman of the Executive Committee. The PNF handles all the PLO's finances according to an annual budget prepared by the Executive Committee and approved by the PNC. The PNF is responsible for developing and overseeing the finances of the PLO, and supervises the finances of the various PLO departments.

3. The Palestine National Liberation Army

In its first session, the PNC resolved that the PLO maintain a regular military force known as the Palestine Liberation Army (PLA). Article 22 of the Basic Law provided for the establishment of "special Palestinian units in accordance with the military needs and the plan to be approved by the United Arab Command and in cooperation with the concerned Arab states."[23]

This article, however, was amended in its entirety at the fourth session of the PNC, held in Cairo in 1968, which was dominated by the growing influence of the Organizations under Fateh's leadership. At this meeting, Fateh alone had 38 of the 100 PNC seats. The Popular Front for the Liberation of Palestine (PFLP) had another 10 seats. Together, the Organizations had 48 seats, or slightly less than 50 percent of the PNC's membership. As a result, the Organizations were able to have passed many significant amendments to the PLO's Charter and Basic Law. Article 22 was amended to read as follows: "The PLO shall form an army of Palestinians, known as the Palestine Liberation Army, with an independent command operating under the supervision of the Executive Committee and executing both specific and general instructions and decisions. Its national duty is to become the vanguard in the battle for liberation of Palestine."[24]

Article 23 specifies that the PLO Executive Committee"shall make every effort to enroll Palestinians in Arab military academies and institutes for military training, to mobilize the potential and resources of the Palestinians, and to prepare them for the battle of liberation."

The name of the Palestine Liberation Army was changed during the 16th PNC session in Algiers in 1983 to the Palestine National Liberation Army (PNLA). This change reflected a consensus among the Organizations to integrate all the various military units of the Palestinian revolution into the PLA.

The relationship between the PLO's political leadership and the PLA's command experienced past periods of tension. The PLA frequently demanded a greater role in the PLO's political decision-making process. For example, in January 1969 the then- PLA chief-of-staff, General Misbah al Budeiri, in a memorandum presented to the Executive Committee of the PLO, rejected the distribution of seats which Fateh had proposed for the forthcoming fourth PNC session.[25]

At that time, the Executive Committee's majority was not yet comprised of the Organizations, although their influence was increasing. In 1976, the same chief-of-staff refused to obey Executive Committee orders to prevent Syrian intervention against the PLO forces in Lebanon. As a result, he was dismissed from his functions the same year. Despite these occasional tensions, the PLA has been kept under control by the PLO's political leadership.

Formerly, the PLA was officially composed of three contingents: the Ain Jalut forces stationed in Egypt; the Qadisiyya forces, originally based in Iraq but transferred to Jordan in June 1967 and finally to Syria, where they are currently stationed; and the Hittin forces stationed in Syria.

The Hittin forces have been the most problematic to the PLO. Despite being officially and technically part of the PLO's army, for all practical purposes it has been under Syrian government control. It has also been used by Syria to implement Syrian policies and, in some cases, against the PLO.

After 1982 the PLA was reconstructed on a new basis. The former PLA and the current PNLA forces have participated in all the battles waged in defense of the Palestinian revolution and the Palestinian people. They participated in the 1967 war waged by Israel against the Arab States; the September 1970 conflict against the Jordanian army; the war of October 1973 alongside the Syrian and the Egyptian armies; in defense of the Palestinian revolution during the 1970s in South Lebanon; against various Israeli military incursions, bombardments and raids; and in Beirut alongside the Lebanese National Movement. During the 1982 siege of Beirut, the PNLA performed heroically in the defense of the city. They have also participated in the defense of the legitimate elected leadership of the PLO and of the Palestinian people during the siege of Tripoli, Lebanon, by Israeli and Syrian forces and their allies, the dissidents from Fateh. Since 1982, the PNLA has repeatedly participated in the defense of the PLO and the Palestinian refugee camps in Lebanon. In recognition of this important role, the PNLA membership in the PNC was raised to 44 members.

It is worth mentioning that the Organizations which constitute the PLO have their own independent military units. Fateh, for example, has the Assifa Forces, which have born the burden of military struggle in the Occupied Territories, protecting Palestinian refugee camps, and defending the PLO's independence in some Arab states, where it faced intervention in its internal affairs. The Assifa Forces have payed dearly in human and material sacrifices and, without its contributions, the PLO would not be what it is today.

The military units of the constituent Organizations operate autonomously and are controlled by their own commands and not by the PLO. However, since 1983, with the reorganization of the PLA, most of these military units have been integrated into the PNLA, especially the Assifa Forces of Fateh.

It is important to emphasize at the conclusion of this section that the PLA/PNLA have never engaged in commando-type activities, contrary to repeated allegations. They have never participated in any military action outside the limited area of operations as defined above.

4. The Political Department

The struggle of the Palestinians to regain their inalienable national rights, as well as their great human and material sacrifices, have earned the Palestinians wide international support. As a result, the PLO enjoys broad recognition as the sole and legitimate representative of the Palestinians throughout Asia, Africa and Latin America, and has strengthened its position in Western public opinion. In November 1974, the PLO's mounting international prestige and the desire of the international community to rectify part of the damage inflicted upon the Palestinians in the aftermath of 1948, led the United Nations to invite Yasser Arafat, as Chairman of the Executive Committee of the Palestine Liberation Organization, to address its General Assembly. This symbolized a significant milestone in the process of international recognition of Palestinian rights and the PLO.

Also, in 1974, the PLO was unanimously recognized as the sole legitimate representative of the Palestinian people at the Arab Summit Conference held in Rabat, Morocco. It has since been recognized by the Organization of African Unity, the Movement of the Non-Aligned Countries and the Organization of the Islamic Conference. The PLO has been granted observer status in the United Nations and participates in the deliberations of the Security Council, according to Rule 37 of the Security Council's Provisional Rules of Procedure. This allows the Security Council to invite the PLO to participate with the same status as any other member of the United Nations which is not a member of the Security Council.[26]The PLO also enjoys observer status in the Organization of African Unity. It is the only non-African state or organization to have been given this status.

It is the responsibility of the PLO's Political Department to represent the organization and the Palestinian people at the international level by conducting all matters regarding relations of the PLO with foreign states or organizations. It essentially acts as the PLO's "ministry of foreign affairs." The Political Department assigns representatives to other countries, and in turn these representatives receive credentials as foreign ambassadors accredited by the PLO. The Political Department is headed by a member of the Executive Committee of the PLO who is assisted by a large departmental staff including a director general and various heads of sections (or desks) responsible for management of political affairs and relations with other states.

In this area of foreign relations, the PLO has scored major successes and achievements. The PLO has come a long way from the time of its establishment when it was only recognized by the League of Arab States, some Arab countries and the Peoples Republic of China. The PLO now has 85 standing representative offices abroad and is accredited in more than 105 states. Of these, 63 states have granted the PLO diplomatic status. Two offices are accredited to the U.N. in New York and Geneva and one to the UNESCO in Paris. All three have observer status typical of a non-member state.

5. The Department for Mass Organizations

The Department for Mass Organizations, headed by a member of the PLO's Executive Committee, is officially responsible for coordination between the different PLO guilds or trade unions and the Executive Committee. Unlike dominant trade unions in many countries—which usually act as umbrella organizations or as a coalition for various specific trade unions in their respective countries—the Palestinian trade unions maintain their organizational, political and financial independence. Some Palestinian unions, like those for students, workers and women, preceded the establishment of the PLO. In fact, the student union, and to a lesser extent the workers' and women's unions, were at one point the only institutions where Palestinians could openly organize and engage themselves in some Arab countries, particularly Egypt, and in some West European countries. That each trade union maintains its organizational, political and financial autonomy underlines the importance Palestinians attach to highlighting the problems of their particular condition.

The primary objective behind the establishment of these unions was political. They satisfy the need to organize political associations for all Palestinians who share a common professional specialization in order to educate and inform their members about the Palestinian situation.

The second objective was to protect the economic and social interests of union members who experienced in many cases political, economical and financial discrimination and who were frequently exploited as cheap labor.

Membership in Palestinian trade unions is high and recruitment has historically been very successful. The Teachers Union, for example, represents 75,000 teachers and instructors working in Arab countries. The Engineers Union has approximately 25,000 members, and the Medical Union counts a membership of 13,000 doctors.[27] Some of these unions have been able to conclude agreements with their host countries, such as in Algeria and Mauritania, to regulate the status of their members. There are 12 unions representing students, laborers, women, teachers, lawyers, doctors and pharmacists, engineers, writers and journalists, farmers, youths and artists. These unions receive their financial support through membership fees, limited financial contributions from the PNF based on PNC decisions, donations and material and financial assistance from Arab countries and friendly trade unions in socialists and western states.

The Palestinian unions' leadership is directly elected by their members according to the democratic principle of one-man, one-vote. The leadership structure in every union includes an elected secretary-general and steering committee, often named the general secretariat, whose membership varies from one union to the other. The highest policymaking organ in these unions is the general congress, which is composed of directly elected representatives from the various branches or units of the particular union. The steering committee (or the general secretariat) is responsible to the general congress. The committee presents its reports and submits its resignation to the congress, which has the power to elect a new steering committee.

Next to the general congress, the second most important policymaking organ is the administrative council of the unions, which meets regularly between sessions of the general congress. This council is composed of the members of the steering committee and representatives from the various branches of each trade union.

Finally, the PLO's Department of Mass Organizations does not interfere in the internal affairs of the unions nor in their democratic processes. It confines its role to purely consultative and coordinating functions.

6. Health, Education, Social and Economic Departments

The PLO has been able to help Palestinians realize their national identity through its political efforts and its cohesive institutional structure. However, the process of Palestinian nation-building would not have been complete without the PLO's efforts in the health, education, culture and economic fields.

The PLO's achievements in these areas reflect the enormity of its efforts and the cultural objectives it sought which left a lasting impact on Palestinian society and beyond.

However, PLO efforts in these fields were hampered by often insurmountable obstacles beyond its control. The most important are the living conditions of the Palestinian people and the existing relations between the PLO and the Arab countries in general, and particularly those hosting Palestinian communities. In developing viable policies in these fields, the PLO has to take into consideration three types of problems:

1. The dispersion of the Palestinian people, of whom 40 percent live under Israeli occupation and 60 percent are refugees.[28] The term refugee is applicable to all Palestinians who are living outside occupied Palestine, whether in UNRWA-built refugee camps in the West Bank, Gaza or elsewhere, or those "integrated" into the societies where they are presently living.

2. As a result of this situation, there are many restrictions imposed on the economic, social, educational and political activities of the Palestinian people resident in Arab countries or inside occupied Palestine.

3. The PLO has had to raise the funds necessary to finance its programs in these fields. Lack of sufficient incoming funds from Arab donor states in accordance with the allotments established at the 1978 Arab Summit meeting in Baghdad complicates the situation further. Despite these financial constraints, however, the PLO has optimized its existing revenue for expenditures on worthy but scaled-down programs. Unfortunately, those most affected by delay or reduced funding are Palestinians inside occupied Palestine.

The Israeli government has never allowed the PLO to directly assist Palestinian social, cultural, economic, health or educational programs or institutions in the Occupied Territories, nor has the PLO been permitted to create such institutions to alleviate some of the vital problems confronting the Palestinian people. However, in cooperation with Jordan, the PLO has channelled funds to existing Palestinian institutions in the Occupied Territories through the joint Jordanian-Palestinian Committee.[29] This has contributed greatly to the development of an infrastructure in the Occupied Territories, specifically in the areas of health care, education and in marketing farming products. This, in turn, has helped to strengthen the steadfastness of the Palestinian people in the Occupied Territories and increase their resistance to unrelenting Israeli practices of destruction to the Palestinian infrastructure. The Committee has extended assistance to all kinds of institutions including health centers, hospitals, schools and universities, social centers, financial institutions, workshops, farmers, contractors, educators, artists, and trade unions and syndicates.

Outside the Occupied Territories, the PLO has become increasingly involved in the social and human needs of the Palestinian people in exile. In the process of its institutional development, the PLO has created several institutions to deal with medical aid and health care, social security, education, and information and economic matters.

a. The Palestine Red Crescent Society[30]

The Executive Committee of the PLO has no established health department. Health and medical functions are largely exercised by the Palestine Red Crescent Society (PRCS), which is the equivalent of the Red Cross or Red Crescent in other states.

The PRCS was established in December 1968, on the eve of the fifth anniversary of the Palestinian revolution. Its creation was motivated by humanitarian considerations and increased concern on the part of the Palestinian revolution for the human dimension of Palestinian life.

The PRCS was originally established by Fateh, or the Palestine National Liberation Movement. It was officially incorporated nine months later into the PLO structure during the sixth session of the PNC held in September 1969 in Cairo, Egypt.

The resolution on "medical services,"[31] adopted by the PNC, gave the PRCS wide-ranging responsibilities. It charged the PRCS with 1) administering medical check-ups for all new recruits in the PLO; 2) providing basic medical training to all PLO fighters in order to create what the resolution termed "the first-aid fighter" and "the soldier nurse"; 3) providing all medical needs including clinics, ambulances and blood banks at forward positions on the confrontation lines; 4) establishing hospital facilities to provide necessary medical treatment to all fighters and their families; the families of martyrs, detainees and prisoners; the Palestinians in refuge camps and frontline towns and villages; and 5) providing for the health needs and social assistance of Palestinians inside the Occupied Territories, in as much as circumstances permit.

The PNC further resolved to consider the PRCS as the only party entitled to receive and organize medical assistance donated by Arab and foreign governments and institutions. The PNC asked the Executive Committee of the PLO to enact laws to regulate and govern PRCS medical personnel. The subsequent regulations stipulated that every new Palestinian graduate of any medical or health institution must serve at least one year with the PRCS. The regulation also calls for the support and assistance of Arab governments in its implementation. Additionally, the PNC asked the PNF to provide a budget to finance the activities of the PRCS, and requested that all organizations cooperate with the PRCS in order to facilitate its duties.

Since then, the PRCS has developed a network of well- organized and sophisticated medical institutions, which provide medical and health care services to all Palestinians, whether civilian or military. These institutions have been established primarily in or near Palestinian population centers and inside the refugee camps. The first PRCS medical and health care institutions were established in Jordan, where the PLO had, at the time, its official main base. Between early 1969 and the departure of Palestinian forces from Jordan following their military conflict with the Jordanian army in 1970-71, the PRCS had established in Jordan eight hospitals, 16 clinics and two recovery centers. After the 1970-71 conflict, all these facilities were closed. Subsequently, the PRCS moved its operations to Lebanon where it underwent fundamental changes and reorganization. Its activities were largely expanded and its facilities and equipment modernized.

The PRCS currently operates 15 major hospitals: nine in Lebanon, four in Syria, one in Egypt and one in North Yemen.[32] Among those in Lebanon is the Akka medical complex, which in itself comprises five hospitals.

In Syria the PRCS has two major medical complexes, the Deir Yassin medical complex in the Yarmouk refugee camp and the Karmel dental complex in Damascus. These centers have a 900-bed capacity in normal circumstances. The number can be doubled in emergencies. Each facility treats approximately 300 cases a day from their outpatient clinics. In addition, the PRCS has 44 major clinics and infirmaries— 14 in Lebanon, 15 in Syria, ten in Egypt, two in Sudan, two in Tunisia and one in Qatar—and a number of postoperatory and recuperation centers in Syria, Lebanon and Tunisia. It also operates a large network of social work centers, and maternal and child-care centers in all the Palestinian refugee camps in Arab host countries.

PRCS hospitals include specialized medical departments such as maternity, pediatrics, orthopedics, dental, obstetrics, general and internal medicine, urology and dermatology. Each facility has its own outpatient clinic and is equipped with modern facilities which include operating theaters, radiology departments, pharmacies, laboratories, blood banks and emergency sections. Some include organic chemistry, bacteriological and parasitological laboratories.

In Lebanon and Egypt, the PRCS runs its own nursing school with a three-year course of registered staff nurses and a two- year course for paramedics. These courses combine both theoretical and practical training.

The majority of physicians employed by PRCS are Palestinians, although there are some from different Arab countries — essentially Lebanon, Iraq, Egypt and Syria — as well as some from European countries including Norway, Sweden, Britain, Finland and France. Highly specialized physicians work under contract for the PRCS.

The PRCS does not operate under normal and relatively peaceful conditions, as do similar institutions in other parts of the world. It is subject to the same general political and military conditions under which the PLO operates. In fact, its medical institutions are extremely vulnerable and have at times been seriously damaged by political developments and events. In many cases, PRCS centers have been closed down or even looted and burned by the enemies of the Palestinians, be they Israeli military forces or sectarian militias.

PRCS institutions came under deliberate attack during the so-called "civil war" in Lebanon in 1975-76. The Red Crescent's main hospital, the Jerusalem Hospital, situated on the Green Line (demarcating the eastern and the western sectors of Beirut) was looted by the Lebanese Phalangist forces. The hospital of Tel al-Zaatar refugee camp in the eastern part of Beirut, as well as other PRCS clinics in this area, were totally destroyed by right- wing Lebanese militias.

During the summer 1982 Israeli invasion of southern Lebanon approximately 200 PRCS personnel, including doctors, nurses, administrative staff and paramedics, were either detained for various periods of time or imprisoned in the Ansar detention camp by the

Israeli army. Furthermore, between the invasion of Lebanon in June 1982 and the second Sabra and Shatila and Burj al-Barajneh massacres in 1985, more than 30 PRCS personnel were killed by the Israeli-allied Phalange and the Syrian-allied Amal militia while on duty carrying out their humanitarian missions.

PRCS institutions were not spared by Israeli land, sea and air bombardments during the summer 1982 siege of Beirut. Despite this situation, the PRCS not only continued its activities, but actually opened new field hospitals inside the besieged city, including the three-story-deep underground field hospital established in the compound of the Anglican Theological College in West Beirut.

Following the Israeli siege and occupation of Beirut in 1982, culminating in the massacres at Sabra and Shatila, PRCS hospitals, clinics and personnel were subjected to killing, rape, looting, arson and destruction. In 1985, as the refugee camps of Sabra, Shatila and Burj al-Barajneh were attacked by Amal militias, PRCS institutions faced a similar campaign of killing, burning and destruction, which did not even spare patients. Additionally, facilities that escaped total destruction were unable to operate, as panicked refugees—both Lebanese and Palestinian—flocked to the hospitals seeking refuge from certain massacre. This was the case at the Akka medical complex in Shatila and the Haifa Hospital in Burj al-Barajneh.

Yet, in spite of all these difficulties, the PRCS never ceased to extend its services to civilian victims regardless of their political or religious loyalties. The PRCS went ahead, as soon as a cease-fire was declared, to rebuild what had been destroyed. Two new hospitals were established in Beirut; the Shatila Hospital in the Shatila refugee camp and the Haifa Hospital in the Burj al-Barajneh refugee camp. In the Ein al- Hilweh refugee camp, on the outskirts of the southern Lebanese city of Saida, the Saad Sayel Hospital was opened. In the Beqaa Valley, the Majid abu Sharar and the Kamal Udwan Hospitals were established inside the Bar Elias and Al-Jaleel refugee camps.

After the PLO's departure from Lebanon in 1982, the PRCS opened hospitals and clinics in the Arab countries which hosted the Palestinian fighters, including Sudan, Iraq, Tunisia and Yemen. The PRCS expanded its presence in Egypt by opening the Ain Shams medical center in Cairo.

The PRCS provides free medical services to all employees of the PLO as well as all members of their families, whether Palestinian or non-Palestinian. Cases which require unavailable specialized treatment are transferred to outside medical facilities at the full expense of the PRCS. Patients who are non-PLO members, whether Palestinian or other Arab nationals among whom the Palestinians live, are charged a nominal fee. Medicine is distributed free of charge from the pharmacies of the PRCS, and are covered by the social security system of the PLO if purchased outside.

The PRCS fulfills another very important function, which is the introduction of preventive medical care service on a large scale, not only within the Palestinian community but also within the Arab states where the Palestinian people reside. This concept developed out of the particularly poor sanitary conditions under which the Palestinian people live in the refugee camps as a result of open sewage and drainage systems, inadequate supply of potable water, unsanitary disposal of waste, extreme overcrowding and poorly constructed shelters which provide inadequate protection from cold winters.[33]

The PRCS not only extends medical care to the injured and the physically disabled, but also provides counseling services to alleviate the psychological consequences of isolation which may befall a newly handicapped person. Rehabilitation is in accordance with a patient's physical and mental capabilities and endeavors to reintegrate individuals as active members of society. For this purpose, the PRCS has opened a number of rehabilitation centers including the Haifa Center which provides medical, health and social services; the Ramleh Physiotherapy and Rehabilitation Center; the Himmeh Physiotherapy and Rehabilitation Center in Damascus; the Dummar Orthopedics Center in the suburbs of Damascus; the Physiotherapy Center of the Jerusalem Hospital in Cairo; and the Ain Shams Center in Cairo for children suffering from polio, deafness, blindness and mental retardation. Before 1982, the PRCS also operated the Nazareth Pediatrics Hospital in Beirut.[34]

Administratively, the PRCS is run by an elected president who is assisted by a board entitled the Executive Council. The Executive Council is the highest policy making body of the PRCS, and it oversees all the activities of the various PRCS institutions. The Red Crescent also has a public relations department which has played an important role in publicizing the PRCS's efforts internationally and in mobilizing support from national and international health and Red Cross societies for PRCS projects.

Since its establishment in 1968, the PRCS has been a member of the International Red Cross Agreement and other international conventions on behalf of the PLO. The PRCS has been granted observer status to the International Committee of the Red Cross, the International League of the Red Cross and the Red Crescent societies. The PRCS also represents the PLO in the World Health Organization, the World Health Assembly and in other international and regional organizations and conferences.

In 1983, the World Health Assembly adopted a resolution affirming "the right of the Palestinian people to have their own humanitarian institutions to provide medical and social services." However, Israel's refusal to cooperate with the World Health Assembly has made it difficult for Palestinians under occupation to establish such institutions in the Occupied Territories. Yet, in spite of the obstacles created by Israel, the PRCS has managed to extend some medical and financial assistance to the existing health organizations and facilities in the West Bank and Gaza.

b. The Department of Education

The Department of Education of the PLO is responsible for the formulation of educational policies and the selection of educational material for PLO-run schools. The department also provides guidance for institutions responsible for the coordination of educational policies. This role is of paramount importance considering the fact that Palestinian children "are subject to curricula that are devoid in content of Palestinian history, culture, and politics..."[35] It cannot be denied that curriculum content has important implications in the process of nation-building and the formation of a national identity. This is particularly applicable in the Palestinian case.

Throughout its existence, the PLO has attempted to organize educational programs for the Palestinians through its Department of Education. In the seventies, the PLO designed a major school program for Palestinians residing in Kuwait and other Gulf countries. It has also cooperated with the Planning Center of the PLO, UNESCO and other Arab institutions in an attempt to establish an open university, adapted to the needs of the Palestinian people. Due to the 1982 Israeli invasion of Lebanon and subsequent logistical complications, this project has yet to be realized.

The Department of Education also administers a scholarship program intended to coordinate and distribute scholarships granted to the PLO by Arab and foreign governments and institutions. The program selects the students eligible for financial assistance and oversees their academic performance.

Considering the importance Palestinians attach to education, this program is of obvious value. The Palestinian emphasis on education is evidenced by the Palestinian literacy rate, which is the highest in the Arab world, and the percentage of Palestinian university graduates, which surpasses even Israel's.

Consistent with its educational policy, the PLO organizes summer programs and courses for Palestinian professionals, students and children in various fields. Over 700 Palestinians have participated in these courses since their inception. In 1984 and 1985, the PLO organized summer courses in computer science for youngsters eight to 16 years of age.

The PLO, through the Department of Education, also serves as administrator for a number of schools in the Middle East. The most important of these is the educational complex in Damascus, Syria. The PLO also runs a number of schools for the children of Palestinian martyrs in Lebanon—such as Abna' al Sumud and Is'ad al Tufula. In Jordan, there is the Beit al-Maqdes school, and in Tunisia, the Abna' al Sumud and the Jerusalem High School.

It is worth noting that until 1982, the PLO Planning Center also had an educational section which served a similar function in drawing up the philosophy and strategy for Palestinian education.

c. The Department of Information, Culture and National Guidance

The struggle against the Israeli occupation of Palestine transcends the military dimension. It is actually a clash between two cultures and civilizations. Israel did not simply occupy the land of Palestine but sought, with the massive power at its disposal, to negate the cultural heritage of the Palestinian people. To that end, it has attempted to usurp Palestinian folklore, including traditional dress, and present them to the world as the product of Israeli culture.[36] Certain Palestinian dishes, which are not necessarily peculiar to Palestine, but characteristic to the whole Arab East, have been misrepresented to the world as native to Israel.

In response to this campaign of distortion and cultural defamation, the PLO created the Department of Information and Culture in 1965. Palestinians have quickly learned that an appreciation of their independent cultural achievements contribute and enrich the development of their national identity as a distinct society which shares a past, a present and a future. A deep awareness of a strong national identity and a dynamic cultural heritage strengthen the adherence of the Palestinian people to the national struggle to regain their homeland.

As a result, the PLO has given serious attention to and support for the development of various organs, institutions and individual artists who articulate or represent Palestinian cultural heritage. The PLO believes that the cultural creativity of any people is a reflection of the strength of its civilization and an honest portrayal of the society's interaction with its heritage. Consequently, the PLO developed the following cultural sections:

Arts and National Culture
Palestine Cinema Institute
The Association for Theater and Palestinian Popular Art
Folklore Dance Troupe
Photography
Sculpture
Graphic Arts
Exhibition Branch
Research Center

Many Palestinian artists have exhibited their works before audiences throughout the world. The Palestinian Folklore Dance Troupe has toured five continents presenting Palestinian and Arab folk music and dance to thousands of people, many of whom were introduced to Arab culture for the very first time.

The PLO has standing exhibition centers for art in museums located throughout the Arab world. The organization's attempts to gather and display Palestinian art suffered a temporary setback during the 1982 Israeli invasion of Lebanon when two of the PLO's major art centers in Beirut, the Sculpture Center and the Al-Karameh Art Gallery, were bombed by Israeli jets.

It is important to mention that this cultural activity is not confined to the Palestinian community. The PLO, with the cooperation of friendly governments and cultural institutions, has succeeded in organizing art exhibitions and competitions focusing on Palestinian themes in foreign countries. Foreign painters, artists, calligraphers and graphic artists have frequently participated in these events. The PLO office in Bolivia, for example, has formalized such activities in an official agreement with the Bolivian government.

Regarding the dissemination of news and information regarding the Palestinians, the PLO has a Bureau of Information which oversees the general political guidelines and information policies followed by the PLO. The Bureau is headed by the Chairman of the Executive Committee who is assisted by representatives from the information offices of the different Organizations represented in the PLO, along with the directors of those offices. The Bureau also oversees the Unified Information Department which includes the Foreign Information Department, the Palestine News Agency (WAFA), the Palestine Cinema and Photography Department, the radio stations, and *Filastin al-Thawra*, the central publication of the PLO.

The Chairman of the Executive Committee of the PLO also heads two other major cultural and policy-oriented bodies: the Planning Center, which was created in the early seventies to present proposals and studies to the Executive Committee; and the Research Center, which was established in 1965 in Beirut.

The Research Center possesses a large library which includes extensive archives. The Center publishes an intellectual monthly journal in Arabic — *Shu'un Filastiniyya* (Palestine Affairs) — along with other Arabic language publications (although a few are in foreign languages). The Center, along with all other Palestinian institutions in Beirut, suffered from flagrant acts of vandalism committed by the Israeli army upon the departure of the PLO from Lebanon in the late summer of 1982. Israeli soldiers entered the offices of the Research Center, looted all movable material, books, papers, documents, archives, furniture and stationery, and transported them to Israel.

Subsequently, in the 1983 negotiations between the PLO and Israel, conducted through the International Red Cross, the PLO insisted that Israel should return intact the entire library stolen from the Research Center along with Palestinian prisoners of war. Israel acquiesced to the PLO demand, and the books were released with the freed Palestinian freedom fighters in December 1983. This marked the first time in the Palestinian-Israeli conflict when libraries and archives were treated as 'prisoners of war' and were exchanged, through international mediation, for captured Israeli soldiers.

d. The Economic Department

Although the Economic Department has been in existence for some time, it did not make its presence felt on the Palestinian political scene until after the 17th session of the PNC in 1984. Since then, the Economic Department has developed an important institution, the Palestinian Bureau of Statistics, based in Damascus, which has regularly published the *Palestinian Statistical Abstract*. The department has also represented the PLO in international economic conferences including those sponsored by the United Nations.

Prior to 1984, the PLO's economic activities were undertaken by other institutions outside the Economic Department. Most such activities were undertaken by the Palestine Martyrs' Sons Work Society, better known as SAMED, the Arabic equivalent for 'steadfast.' In 1984, however, after the 17th PNC session, the Economic Department was reorganized to include SAMED and its various offices. The president of SAMED then became the director general of the Economic Department.

SAMED originally had a specific social function when it was created in 1970 in Jordan as a modest organization of small workshops and vocational training centers. Its goal was to provide vocational training for the widows and the children of those who had lost their lives in service to the Palestinian cause. SAMED was meant to help these children and their families find adequate housing, give them vocational training, provide them with job opportunities, and guarantee them an income which would enable them to enjoy a productive and dignified life.

With the departure of the Palestinian military forces from Jordan in 1970, SAMED was forced to move to Lebanon. There, it was totally reorganized, and grew from a small venture with a capital of only $6,000,[37] into a multi-faceted economic organization with institutions and branches spread over 30 nations in four continents[38] and possessing a total investment capacity of approximately $50 million[39].

In his opening statement at the Third Congress of SAMED, Chairman Yasser Arafat described the organization as "a commercial institution not solely motivated by considerations of profit and loss."[40] Its director general, Mr. Abu 'Ala' describes the organization in these words: "SAMED is not an investment project which aims at realizing maximum economic returns...SAMED is the economic arm of the Palestinian revolution and the nucleus of its public sector...It is committed to the political line and program of the PLO. Its workers are militants within the framework of the PLO."[41] (It is) "a unique human experience in the history of all national liberation movements" (because it has been assigned the task of forming) "a public sector and establishing the nucleus of a Palestinian national economy."[42]

Chairman Arafat was even more explicit in his definition of the functions of SAMED by stating that the organization is necessary in the process of setting up "the future state" of Palestine as well as in the future establishment of the "Jordanian-Palestinian Confederation."[43]

The multiple objectives of SAMED are, indeed, ambitious. They include:

1. training the sons of Palestinian martyrs and providing them with job opportunities;

2. providing jobs for residents of Palestinian refugee camps;

3. participating in the social and economic development of Palestinian communities;

4. achievement of self-sufficiency in the essential needs of the Palestinian revolution and the Palestinian masses by developing a nucleus for a national Palestinian industry and the provision of adequate economic commodities with affordable prices within the reach of the widest possible section of Palestinian society;

5. the restructuring of the Palestinian national economy through the establishment of public industrial, agricultural and commercial enterprises and training an administrative and technical cadre capable of assuming control over and managing the above-mentioned establishments;

6. the creation of a nucleus for a Palestinian public sector, taking into account the peculiar Palestinian situation and exploiting all available opportunities;

7. providing support for Palestinian people in the occupied homeland through all possible means;

8. participating in the development of industrial, agricultural and commercial investments through joint projects with Arab, African and Asian countries; and

9. enhancement of Palestinian international relations through joint economic cooperation with other parties.[44]

SAMED also serves an ideological function as it attempts to create the nucleus of a "Palestinian working class which believes in the revolution and is always ready to make sacrifices for it, cooperate with it and binds its destiny to it."[45]

When Arafat described SAMED as not "solely motivated by considerations of profit and loss," he was in fact stating that the objective behind the establishment of SAMED was not based purely on commercial or economic considerations, but also included political considerations.

The establishment of SAMED was originally a decision made within Fateh. For this reason, it continues to rely on Fateh for assistance concerning its numerous financial and economic problems. SAMED's institutions and offices have been partly or completely destroyed, as have those of the PRCS, whenever the Palestinians have faced military aggression. Whether in 1970-71 in Jordan, during the 1976-82 civil strife in Lebanon, during the heavy Israeli bombardment of Beirut in the summer of 1982, or during the massacres perpetrated by the Amal militias in 1985 against the Palestinian refugee camps in Beirut, SAMED suffered extensive losses. SAMED's losses as a result of the Israeli aggression alone are estimated at 77 million Lebanese pounds (the equivalent of $17 million).[46] The Director General of SAMED estimates its losses resulting from the "war of the camps" in 1985 at $14 million.[47]

Despite recurrent campaigns of aggression and destruction and the continuing instability of the Lebanese polity, the Fateh Central Committee has decided to rebuild the destroyed institutions. Chairman Arafat confirmed this decision in his speech to SAMED's Third Congress. According to SAMED's Board of Directors, his instructions were explicit: "The destroyed SAMED institutions must be rebuilt as soon as Israel withdraws from the territories it occupies in order to serve the immediate needs of the Palestinians. The reconstruction of SAMED's Beirut-based institutions must begin immediately. Employees of SAMED are to return to their jobs immediately. As long as SAMED's facilities are still under reconstruction, all SAMED employees would be treated as Fateh cadre. This meant that Fateh would pay employee salaries throughout the rebuilding process."[48]

Chairman Arafat's directives were based on his concern for families financially dependent on SAMED incomes. Of SAMED's 3,000 workers in Lebanon, 2,000 are women and their salaries are a necessity to the financial stability of many Palestinian families.[49]

To achieve its objectives SAMED operates in industry, agriculture, trade and marketing, construction, film production, information and culture, publishing and distribution, research and studies, and finance and management. The headquarters of SAMED, now based in Amman, Jordan, assumes the responsibility of supervising the organization's various activities by overseeing the specialized departments and extending assistance to sister- organizations which operate in the above-mentioned fields. The activities of SAMED are more fully listed below:

The Industrial Department

SAMED's industries produce ready-made clothes, textiles, wool, blankets, furniture, technical and advertising products, food products, sanitary towels, construction equipment, embroidery, and plastic products.

At its peak, SAMED incorporated 43 industries employing a total of 3,489 Palestinians. These included 2,008 full-time workers and 1,481 part-time employees. Though many of these industries were destroyed in 1982, most have since been reconstructed.[50]

Faced with heavy losses in 1982, the directors of SAMED met in an extraordinary meeting in early 1983 in Budapest, Hungary, to review the losses and the prospects of continuing their work. In light of the decision of Fateh's Central Committee and the clear instructions of Chairman Arafat, they decided to reorganize SAMED and to seek the assistance and cooperation of a number of Arab and foreign countries. Consequently, SAMED's industrial activities were resumed and extended to include projects for the production of ready-made clothes and furniture in South Yemen, facilities for ready-made clothes and house appliances in North Yemen, and joint projects in other fields in Romania, Poland, Thailand and Egypt.

Department of Trade and Marketing

SAMED also undertakes the responsibility of marketing industrial and farm products. This is done through the following sub-divisions:

Permanent and Temporary Showrooms

SAMED has established 26 permanent showrooms in 14 Arab and African countries including Algeria, Lebanon, South Yemen, North Yemen, the United Arab Emirates, Libya, Djibouti, Sudan and Somalia.[51] In Africa, it has showrooms in Brazzaville, Congo; Conakry, Guinea; Mali; and Tanzania. SAMED has plans to open showrooms in Saudi Arabia, Senegal, Nigeria and Egypt. It also has been invited to open showrooms in Angola, Burkina Fasso, Zambia and Zimbabwe. Discussions are underway to open showrooms in the German Democratic Republic, Hungary, Poland, the Soviet Union, the United States, Canada and in various Latin American states.

These showrooms not only display the work of SAMED, but also help to market industrial, agricultural and artistic products from the Occupied Territories. The exhibits also play a secondary role by introducing to the public the social and economic activities of the Palestinian people.[52]

Trade Offices

SAMED has opened 20 offices to facilitate trade with many countries in Africa, Asia (Japan, Thailand and China), Latin America, the socialist countries and Western Europe. In addition to facilitating trade, these offices prepare feasibility studies on economic and commercial activities as well as on the transfer of modern equipment and technology to SAMED factories and workshops.

Joint Ventures

In 1975, SAMED began to establish joint economic ventures with friendly states. These ventures deal with farm products, construction, finance, agriculture, industry, film production, printing, publishing and distribution.

International Exhibitions

SAMED represents the PLO in 44 international exhibitions where it displays its own products and those it markets from the Occupied Territories. Though SAMED initially only participated in the political and cultural exhibits, it has recently expanded its participation to other areas.

Agriculture and Agricultural Production

The PLO's decision to establish agricultural projects in a number of African and Arab countries was partially political, aimed at increasing cooperation and solidarity between the Palestinian people and the population of the countries involved. SAMED faced many problems in the initial stages of this effort due to the archaic state of the agricultural sector in many participating countries and the continuing impact of the colonialist era on local agriculture. Nevertheless, concentrated efforts were spent on developing the agricultural sector in several countries through the following projects:

SAMED Agricultural Project (Sudan) The area of the project is 2,300 acres. It was established in 1983 and it produces lemons, mangoes and some field crops.

Palestine Farm (Somalia) Its area is 815 acres and it produces sesame and bananas.

Palestine Friendship Farm (Guinea) Its area is 4,500 acres and it produces mangoes and pineapple. A poultry farm is attached to the project.

SAMED Solidarity Farm (Guinea Bissau) Its area is 1,730 acres and it produces pineapple, avocado, bananas, citrus and mangoes.

Palestine Farm (Iraq) Its area is 750 acres. It is still in the first stages of reclamation and includes a poultry farm.

Other farms are operated in North Yemen, Syria, Uganda, Egypt, Lebanon and Mali. The collective area of the farms is around 12,500 acres. These sites produce guava, mangoes, papaya, corn and rice. Sheep and cattle are also raised on these farms. All of these agricultural projects are jointly supervised by Palestinian agricultural engineers and local experts from the countries where the farms are situated.

A large percentage of the foreign aid given by the PLO to friendly countries is channelled through SAMED, although other institutions and departments of the PLO have their own foreign aid programs, the most important of which is the medical assistance given by the PRCS.

Research and Publication Department

SAMED has cooperated with a number of research institutes to study the history of the Palestinian labor movement in Palestine including work conditions in the Israeli-occupied territories and outside Palestine. The department publishes a monthly theoretical economic journal entitled *Samed al-Iqtisadi*. In Beirut, SAMED operated its own publishing house until 1982. In the following years, it resumed its research and publishing activities and established the SAMED Studies and Publishing House in Amman in cooperation with the Al-Karmel Publishing and Distribution House.

Department for Film Production

The Departmeent for Film Production, established in 1976, was expanded in 1980 through the addition of highly sophisticated film production and sound technology sections. Though hindered by the 1982 Israeli invasion, SAMED was nevertheless able to produce several major films which received awards in documentary film festivals throughout the world. Among these films are *The Key, The Day of the Land and The Olive Branch.*

SAMED also co-produced a film on the Israeli settlements in the Occupied Territories and another on the Palestinian resistance to Israeli occupation. SAMED is planning several new feature films and is contemplating a number of television productions on the cultural aspects of the Palestinian question.

International economic relations of the PLO also fall within SAMED's domain. Chairman Arafat stated that the Executive Committee of the PLO had decided that "SAMED undertake to develop the economic relations between the PLO and friendly countries throughout the developing world."[53] Since that decision was adopted, SAMED has negotiated and ratified a number of economic and technical agreements for cooperation with other countries. For example, it has signed agreements with Mali, Tanzania, the German Democratic Republic, Poland and Hungary. These agreements constitute a precedent in international economic relations.[54] When SAMED signed a technical and economic agreement with the German Democratic Republic, the Minister of Foreign Trade of the G.D.R. described the uniqueness of the agreement clearly:

"Neither my government, nor for that matter any government,

has concluded an agreement of this magnitude with any liberation movement. We are fully conscious of the significance of concluding this agreement. We know with whom we are signing the agreement and why. We are signing with the PLO. We want to extend our recognition of the PLO from the political level to the territorial one."[55]

The significance and importance of signing trade, economic and technical cooperation agreements with the PLO has also been recognized by other socialist countries. The successful conclusion of such agreements with the PLO not only underline the importance and reliability of SAMED as an effective partner, but it is also a clear indication of the level of support that the PLO receives on the international level, particularly since many of these agreements came at crucial landmarks in recent PLO history. Hungary, for example, signed such an agreement at the end of October 1983, at a time when the leadership of the PLO, under the Chairmanship of Yasser Arafat, was subjected to military pressure from Syrian-backed forces in a desperate drive to force the PLO from its last base in Lebanon in the northern city of Tripoli. Poland signed another agreement with the PLO in November 1984 at the closing of the 17th session of the PNC which was subject to a great deal of contention among the different PLO factions. The ratification of these agreements indicated the concrete solidarity of these nations with the struggle of the Palestinian people under the leadership of the PLO.

The Judicial Branch

The Judicial branch plays an important role in the governing process of any society. The Palestinian community is not an exception to this rule. However, while judiciaries function unhampered in countries with a democratic environment and a territorial base, the Palestinian judiciary must make allowances for the unique circumstances of the diaspora.

The development of this branch, within the state-like infrastructure of the PLO, did not proceed at the same pace as that of other Palestinian institutions due to the particular nature of the Palestinian condition. As a stateless people residing in different host countries, the Palestinians are subject to the existing judicial order in their respective places of residence. Under Israeli occupation, for example, Palestinians are governed by a judicial system based on Israeli and Jordanian law.

Outside the Occupied Territories, Palestinians come under the jurisdiction of the judicial system of the specific Arab host countries in which they reside. It was agreed at the time of the establishment of the PLO that even the PLA would be subject to the judicial system applicable to the armed forces on whose territory the PLA is stationed.

In spite of this complex situation, the PLO initiated its own judicial system in 1968 when it created the Supreme Court of the Revolution. The formal institutionalization of the judicial system, however, had to wait until the late seventies when its infrastructure began to take shape. In July 1979, Chairman Arafat signed a decree adopting the Revolutionary Codes of Procedure of the PLO, the Revolutionary Penal Code of the PLO, the Prisons and Reformatory Centers Code of the PLO, and the regulation of Revolutionary Court fees in the PLO.[56]

The adoption of these decrees marked the culmination of a long process of practice and experience in which the PLO dealt with the various legal matters relevant to the Palestinian people in the diaspora. The laws were necessitated by the fact that the PLO was responsible for the protection of the various interests of the Palestinian community. Prior to this date, the application of due process of law within the PLO was based on the set of laws Fateh adopted in 1974 for its revolutionary courts. Factors relevant to this process include the state of the Palestinian revolution, the security situation resulting from this stage of the national liberation struggle, the moral and political principles of the revolution and the necessity of harmoniously coexisting with the laws of the host Arab countries.

In his introduction to *Collection of the Penal Laws of the PLO*, Brigadier General M.T. Al-Russan, the head of the Palestinian Judiciary Department, outlines the reasons for which these laws were codified. He states that first, such a codification serves to define and classify the types of crimes and criminals that they may be referred to the appropriate courts where they may be tried in accordance with established principles of justice. Second, there exists a need to secure the right of competent defense for the accused. Third, such codification serves to unify the penal codes for all the Fedayeen organizations in the PLO. Finally, they also serve to protect the PLO and the Palestinians by deterring potential criminals from committing acts harmful to society. Thus, punishment not only has a punitive function but a deterrent and corrective one as well. It is a means of eradicating crime and its causes simultaneously.

Despite the fact that this study cannot deal at length with the institutions of the Judiciary Branch or with the legal theory and development of these institutions, it is necessary to discuss the major guidelines behind these four codes of law.

1. *The Revolutionary Codes of Procedure*

The 358 articles of this law detail the codes of procedure which define the function of the Attorney General and his deputies and agents and their duties and methods of conducting investigations. Most importantly, this law provides for the right of the accused to adequate defense.

The law also provides a number of guarantees which protect the individual against judicial errors. These guarantees enable the defendant to use all legal methods in the interest of justice. Thus, the law provides that the accused has the right to legal counsel of his own choosing. If the defendant lacks the means to hire legal counsel, or cannot locate one, the court then has the responsibility of assigning legal counsel of which the defendant approves. The law also stipulates that investigations must be completed within three days or referred to a competent tribunal, and that the court proceedings be public in order to guarantee a fair hearing of the case.

The judgment passed has a corrective more than a punitive function. Furthermore, the accused has the right of appeal to a higher tribunal if he is not satisfied with the judgment. Once executed by the court, a judgment has to be referred to the higher authorities for ratification, clemency, or mitigation.

The law also provides that no person shall be detained for more than 24 hours without the authorization of the Attorney General. It also prohibits the entering of private property by the agents of the judiciary without a warrant from the Attorney General. The Palestinian judicial system, however, has not adopted the concept of trial by jury.

The law subdivides the Revolutionary Court system into a Central Court, Special Courts and Military Courts. The law outlines the procedures and the competence of these courts. It stipulates that the accused is entitled to a speedy trial without jeopardizing in any way the course of the trial or the rights of the defendant. This is primarily aimed at protecting the accused from any psychological trauma which might arise from unnecessary delay in the judicial proceedings. It also aims at establishing, in the mind of the accused, a link between the crime committed and the punishment pronounced. This is the objective of deterrence. The law also outlines the procedures for appeal or review by a higher tribunal.

There are also codified laws applicable to military personnel who breach the law. These laws empower military commanders with the right to hear and investigate potential violations and discipline those involved.

It is the prerogative of the Highest Ratification Authority in the PLO to ratify or reject the judgment of the courts. The Authority can either ratify the sentence, reduce it, or pardon the defendant. It cannot, however, throw out the verdict in order to impose a harsher sentence. The rejection of the verdict requires that the case be referred, once again, to the court. If the court determines the innocence of the accused, the Authority has to ratify the sentence, but if the court decides otherwise, the Authority has the right to use its powers in the interest of the accused.

Most important, the law provides for the independence of the judiciary branch. It stipulates explicitly that the Palestinian Revolutionary Judiciary Department is one of the institutions of the PLO. The department is exclusively managed by an administrator who is assisted by a departmental staff without outside interference. The head of the department is the highest competent authority in matters of administration, guidance, and supervision of the many responsibilities assigned to the department. He discharges his functions according to law and reports directly, and only on administrative matters, to the Chairman of the Executive Committee of the PLO and the commander-in-chief of the forces of the Palestinian revolution.

This law also deals with other legal issues such as forgery, testimony of witnesses, false imprisonment, clemency, and conflicts between public and private law.

2. The Revolutionary Penal Code

The 468 articles of this law prohibit physical, psychological or political pressure and intimidation, and all forms of torture. The law also forbids any infringement on personal liberties. It deals with crimes which threaten the public order or public facilities, including the properties of the PLO.

The law prohibits the forgery of documents, protects private and public property, forbids financial and commercial embezzlement and any obstruction of friendly relations and cooperation between the PLO and foreign states and peoples. Article 162 of the Penal Code stipulates prison sentences for such crimes as kidnapping or the hijacking of a plane, train, boat or other property.

The law also strictly prohibits any form of discrimination based on racial, ethnic, religious, regional or national grounds. The law further protects the security and the well-being of the Palestinian people, the PLO and the revolutionary armed forces by providing for the protection of the PLO from foreign aggression, internal secession and military coups. To that end, the law made the usurpation of political, civilian, or military posts a punishable crime.

3. *The Prisons and Reformatory Centers Code*

This law, which includes 140 articles, is based on the premise that prisons are not merely places of detention for those who breach the law. They are centers for the rehabilitation of criminals, in order to help prisoners recover their sense of civil responsibility and to promote their future adherence to codes of conduct, which conform to the accepted public values of a civilized society.

The concept of establishing and operating these centers is influenced a *contrario* by the inhumane treatment and conditions represented by the repression and torture practiced against Palestinian prisoners in Israeli jails. The PLO seeks to provide more humane and civilized treatment to prisoners accused and convicted of breaching the law or those who are prisoners of war.

The law guarantees prisoners the right to receive reading material including books, educational material and newspapers. Prisoners are also legally entitled to receive religious, educational, ethical and political instruction, in addition to appropriate vocational training.

In contrast to the Israeli legal practice of mass detention (a method of revenge against the Palestinian population living under occupation for acts of resistance against Israeli occupation), the laws of the PLO stipulate that punishment is personal. The responsibility for committing a crime lies solely with the culprit who is convicted of that specific violation of the law. His family, relatives or neighbors do not share that responsibility before the law.

Furthermore, the law provides that each prisoner is entitled to half of his monthly salary and to all family allowances and social benefits, regardless of the gravity of the crime and the nature of the verdict rendered in the case. This procedure is aimed at protecting the family of the prisoner against poverty and other social hardships.

4. *Regulation of Revolutionary Court Fees in the PLO*

According to the stipulations of the 28 articles which constitute this law, prisoners are exempted from paying living expenses during their period of detention and from paying all other costs which they might incur during the process of rehabilitation. Prisoners are exempted from paying court fees, as well.

Conclusion

The PLO has been successful, over the past 23 years, in developing a state-like structure based on democracy, freedom of expression and thought, pluralism, and the principle of free discussion and deliberations. Some of its institutions were established in 1964, others were developed as dictated by daily Palestinian needs throughout a natural process of institutional maturation. The primary consideration underlying the PLO's organizational framework is based on the principle of internal checks and balances provided by an independent legislative branch, an effective executive branch and a free judicial system.

The process is yet to be completed. The Palestinian people still do not reside in their homeland under their own government. Nevertheless, the present structure reflects the dreams and hopes of the Palestinian people and their common understanding of the nature of their future state.

Today, the PLO enjoys widespread international recognition and prestige as the sole legitimate representative of the Palestinians. It has been recognized as such by 105 nations. Presently, more states recognize and have diplomatic relations with the PLO than with Israel.

The PLO differs, by its very nature, from other organizations which have represented or still represent their respective peoples in struggles for national liberation. The PLO is not merely a political party or even a liberation front. It is an institution which has a state-like nature. It has also been described as a framework within which different mass organizations and independent individuals operate.

As such, it can be said objectively that the PLO is now the institutional framework for the Palestinian national identity. This function is usually undertaken by the institution of the nation-state in other societies. Thus, the PLO is simply an organization susceptible to internal divisions and splits. It is the institutional framework of a state which incorporates a diversity of trends and attitudes.

Political identification, or the sense of belonging that one has vis-as-vis his homeland, finds its institutional expression in the state. The state, in turn, serves as a frame of reference to all those who are classified as citizens, i.e., all those who share the same rights and duties within the framework of the state. Thus, attachment to the state coincides with attachment to the national homeland. In the case when the state is temporarily absent for any reason, the citizens wage a struggle for self-determination in their attempt to exercise national sovereignty. The PLO provides the framework through which this is accomplished.

The PLO acquired this unique character as a result of the unique status of the Palestinian struggle which differs, in many ways, from other modern national conflicts. The PLO is more than a national liberation movement; its scope is larger than an anti- racist movement and it is more than a struggle against alien settlers. It is all of these, but at the same time more than their sum total. The PLO is forced to address the circumstances created by Israel's deportation of more than half of the Palestinian people from their homes, its denial of the very identity of the remaining half, and its refusal to acknowledge the historical reality of Palestine by negating its past, present and future.

Because of the totality of Israeli attempts to wipe the Palestinian existence from reality, the initial Palestinian dispersion of 1948 is called the "Catastrophe." There is nothing in contemporary political literature which adequately depicts that national trauma. The enemies of the Palestinians have sought to destroy them as a people and to extinguish their identity. This fact explains the top priority the Palestinian struggle has assigned to efforts to reaffirm this identity and to reorganize Palestinian life on all levels.

The process of establishing, developing and maintaining the PLO has not been as easy as the establishment, development, and maintenance of governmental institutions in stable countries in full control of their national territory. The former process necessitates a compensation for the absence of land, i.e., a national territory, by accelerating the struggle to regain it. Thus, the armed struggle waged by the Palestinian people is not only a necessity imposed upon them by their objective conditions, it is also a means of expressing their national identity. Half of the Palestinian population are refugees, while the other half are under occupation. Anyone who ceases the struggle for liberating Palestine, even on a temporary basis, ceases to be Palestinian.

Many Palestinians do not possess any official identity papers which indicate their nationality. This means that the Palestinians do not have an official institution which issues passports to Palestinian citizens. Some Palestinians, for practical or logistical reasons, carry passports issued by countries other than Palestine. What defines the identity of every Palestinian, irrespective of the papers he may hold, is his "belonging" to the PLO, though he or she might not hold membership in any of its specific constituent groups or institutions. In this sense, and in the absence in Palestine of an internationally recognized homeland for the Palestinian people, the PLO becomes the national framework of the Palestinians.

In 1948, the year of the "Catastrophe," the Palestinian people were dispersed throughout many countries. Since then, they have often lived in communities cut off from one another for long periods of time. In the absence of common institutions, it has become only logical that there emerged among Palestinians a multiplicity of political visions, attitudes and positions, though the orientation towards Palestine remained a common one. This multiplicity of approaches is common to all societies, with partisans of each approach interacting within the framework of the national homeland and its institutions.

This absence of a homeland and of common national institutions contributed to disunity and weakness. Initially, the PLO was established as a response to the Palestinian need to translate their aspirations into a concrete framework within which different opinions could interact in harmony. Therefore, in addition to being the symbol of Palestinian identity, the PLO is also the framework through which the national unity of the Palestinian people is expressed.

Each society has its superstructure and infrastructure. It is the superstructure which is forced to make fundamental adjustments when political change takes place. The infrastructure is affected to a lesser extent. With very few exceptions, the institutions such as health, social, educational and economic services continue to function on a daily basis. Since 1948, however, the Palestinian superstructure and infrastructure have been forced to accommodate the realities of Israeli occupation. The PLO has worked to rebuild and redefine both the superstructure and the infrastructure as necessary to promote the welfare of the Palestinian people and to compensate for the political and social loss which they have suffered. Hence, the PLO is not merely a political organization, nor is it only the leadership of the Palestinian struggle in all its facets, including the military one. It is also the institutional framework which incorporates the different social institutions which have developed to service the Palestinian people.

Due to the unique role of the PLO, it also has a unique organizational setup. The Palestine National Council, representing all segments of the Palestinian people, has supreme authority in the PLO hierarchy. This Council elects the other leading bodies of the PLO, such as the Executive Committee and the Central Council. The remaining departments and specialized organs derive their authority from the PNC.

Those who question the authenticity of the relationship between the PLO and the Palestinian people are confusing the nature and role of the PLO, with those of ordinary political organizations such as political parties. Over the years, a large number of international delegations have traveled to occupied Palestine on fact-finding missions. All of them have come back convinced that the vast majority, if not all, of the Palestinians consider the PLO their sole legitimate representative. No ordinary political party or organization enjoys this degree of explicit support.

This underscores the fact that loyalty to the PLO is also an expression of attachment to the Palestinian homeland. It logically follows that all political activism and resistance in the Occupied Territories center fundamentally around public attachment and allegiance to the PLO and rejection of attempts to deprive it of its central role in shaping their political future.

For this reason, Israeli policy has consistently sought to undermine the power base of the PLO inside occupied Palestine. These Israeli attempts have failed miserably. This failure is the outcome of Palestinian Arab steadfastness and resistance since 1948. The Israeli authorities continue to express surprise when Palestinian Arabs hoist the Palestinian national flag despite almost 40 years of intimidation, oppression and terror.

The adoption of a position towards the PLO is not simply a matter of supporting a legitimate national liberation movement or choosing to back one organization among many. It is, instead, an acceptance of the right of the Palestinian people to freely express their national identity and aspirations through the PLO. Those who doubt that the PLO is actually the sole legitimate representative of the Palestinian people have never been able to come up with an alternative. Furthermore, Palestinians argue that the question of representation is an internal matter that should be left for the Palestinians to decide democratically and free of outside intervention.

It is in the interest of world peace and in the interest of the international community to assist the Palestinians in regaining their inalienable national rights as recognized by the United Nations, which represents international legality.

The Palestinians have made significant contributions to the search for peace in the Middle East. The PLO has put forward a number of proposals aimed at furthering a peaceful settlement to the conflict. The words of Yasser Arafat, Chairman of the Executive Committee of the PLO, uttered before the United Nations General Assembly in November 1974, are as valid today as then when he appealed to the world community: "I come to you today with the olive branch in one hand and the rifle of the revolution in the other. Do not make me drop the olive branch...." Those who assume responsibility for world peace should never allow that to happen. The search for a just and comprehensive peace must go on.

FOOTNOTES

1. See the statement of former Israeli Defense Minister Ariel Sharon to U.S. envoy Philip Habib and U.S. charge d'affaires in Israel William Brown on December 5, 1981, in Ze'ev Schiff and Ehud Ya'ari, *Israel's Lebanon War* (New York: Simon and Schuster, 1984), p. 66. Some weeks later, during his trip to the United States, Sharon reiterated the same position in front of the then U.S. Secretary of State, Alexander Haig, see Schiff and Ya'ari, ibid., p. 73.

Two weeks after the start of the Israeli invasion of Lebanon Sharon underlined this objective in an interview with *Ma'ariv* (Israeli daily) on June 18, 1982. For a translation of this interview in Arabic see the Institute of Palestine Studies, Hebrew Section, *The Israeli War in Lebanon, June-December 1982: A Selection of Reports, Documents and Articles From the Hebrew Press.* (Nicosia, Cyprus: Independent Publication Services Ltd., 1983), p. 43.

2. Institute for Palestine Studies, *International Documents on Palestine, 1978.* (Beirut), pp. 192-196; and Chairman Arafat's comments on this statement in ibid., pp. 491-493, 564-566 and 611-615.

3. "Shultz Tells Arabs to Dump PLO," *Philadelphia Inquirer*, April 12, 1983, and "Reagan Assails Arab Radicals, Deplores' 'Peace Veto,' Shultz criticizes PLO," *Los Angeles Times*, April 13, 1983.

4. For a detailed study on this subject see George J. Tomeh, "When the UN Dropped the Palestine Question," *Journal of Palestine Studies*, Vol. IV, no. 1 (Autumn 1974); pp. 15-30. The question of Palestine was dropped from the agenda of the UN Security Council in May 1967. Ibid., pp.25-26.

5. *Assabah* (Tunisian daily newspaper), March 13, 1986, p. 8.

6. By 1965 there were 40 other organizations competing for Palestinian allegiance according to Ghassan Kanafani in the Palestinian supplement of *Al Muharrir*, December 30, 1965 as quoted in Rashid Hamid's, "What is the PLO?" *Journal of Palestine Studies (16)*, Vol. IV, no. 4 (Summer 1975): p. 93.

7. These are referred to in Cheryl Rubenberg's, *The Palestine Liberation Organization: Its Institutional Infrastructure*, (Belmont, MA: Institute of Arab Studies, 1983), p. 6.

8. The important issues of substance which warrant a two-third majority

in the voting procedure of the PNC are: the quorum; amendment of the PLO Charter; amendment of the Basic Law of the PNC; amendment, changes, or annulment of a previously adopted decision or resolution of the PNC and loss of membership in the PNC.

9. A detailed analysis of the amended articles of the Charter and the Basic Law and comparison between the 1964 and 1968 sessions of the PNC is available in Rashid Hamid's. ed., *Resolutions of the Palestine National Assembly 1964-1974* [Arabic]. (Beirut: PLO Research Center, 1975), pp. 19-27. Also in Hamid's, "What is the PLO?" pp. 98-101.

10. Khaled al Hasan, *The Jordanian Palestinian Accord for Joint Action in the Light of the Basic Principles for Political Decision and Action*. (Arabic) (Kuwait: Al Anbaa Press, 1985), p.87.

11. Ibid.

12. In 1986, the Democratic Front, and the coalition list of the Popular Front and the Communist Party lost in the student council elections at the universities of Al-Najah in Nablus and at Bir Zeit University two weeks earlier. Fateh-supported lists were able to form the Student Council. See: *Filastin al Thawra,* no. 592, 1 February 1986, p. 16. However, when these organizations ran with Fateh on a national unity list during the election for the General Union of Palestinian Students in Aden, the result of the elections was that Fateh won four seats and the other organizations (The Popular Front, the Democratic Front and the Palestine Liberation Front) received one seat each. See *WAFA* (The Palestine News Agency) April 19, 1986, p. 10.

13. All references to the Charter and Fundamental Laws of the PLO are taken from the official text published in January 1979 by the PLO. The official text also includes the "Internal Regulations" or "By-laws of the PNC." At the second session of the PNC held in Cairo, Egypt, in June 1965, a detailed electoral law was passed. For text see: Hamid, *Resolutions of the Palestine National Assembly, 1964-1974* [Arabic], (Beirut: PLO Research Center, 1975), pp. 80-87.

14. Ibrahim Abu Lughod, "The Role of the PLO," paper presented to the UN Seminar on the Question of Palestine, April 1985, p. 33.

15. *Al' Muharrir*, December 28, 1966, as quoted in Hamid, "What is the PLO?" p. 97.

16. Judith Miller,"The PLO in Exile," and "The PLO Investment Portfolio," in *New York Times Magazine*, August 18, 1985. Ernie Meyer, "Rewards of Terror," *The Jerusalem Post*, November 23, 1985, p. 14. *The Times* (London), December 9, 1985, p. 14.

17. "The Report of the PNF," *The PLO's PNC, The Seventeenth Session from November 22nd to 29th 1984*, Amman, Jordan (1985), p. 95.

18. Ibid.

19. Ibid., p. 115.

20. Ibid., p. 95.

21. Ibid., pp. 95-96.

22. It must be noted here that Mr. Salah Khalaf (Abu Iyad), a member of the Fateh Central Committee, declared in an interview in late March 1986 that the president of the United Arab Emirates ordered his government to

pay its financial commitments to the PLO as of the first of March 1986.
He thanked also the government of Saudi Arabia for being prompt in paying its shares. Mr. Khalaf also said, that Iraq, despite its war with Iran, has
paid all its financial commitments that accrued in 1985. See interview in
Al-Sharq Al-Awsat (Saudi daily newspaper published in London) March 26,
1986, p. 3.

23. Hamid, *Resolutions*. p. 53.

24. Ibid., p. 121.

25. Ibid., p. 126.

26. These are the words of the U.S. representative serving as president of
the UN Security Council for the month of October 1985, explaining his
vote against the invitation of Mr. Farouk Kaddoumi, Head of the Political
Department of the PLO, to participate in the deliberations of the Security
Council. The U.S. representative wanted to invite the PLO according to rule
39 on the basis of which "the Security Council may invite members of the
Secretariat or other persons whom it considers competent for the purpose,
to supply it with information or to give other assistance in examining matters within its competence." The U.S. "...would certainly not object" to the
participation of the PLO in the Security Council deliberations, "had this
matter been ruled under that rule [39]", the American representative stated.
Rule 37 states, however, that "any member of the United Nations who is
not a member of the Security Council may be invited to participate, without
vote, in the discussion of any question brought before the Security Council
when the Security Council considers that the interests of that member are
specially affected, or when a member brings a matter to the attention of
the Security Council, in accordance with Article 35 (1) of the Charter". The
council decided to invite the PLO despite U.S. objections, according to rule
37, as it has always done ever since the PLO joined the United Nations in
1975.

27. Khaled al-Hasan "The Role of the Palestine Liberation Organization
in the Social, Cultural, Economic and Political Development of the Palestinian People and in the Attainment of its Political Objectives," a paper
presented at the UN seminar on the Question of Palestine, Tunis, August
14-18, 1984, document No. TUN/SEM/1984/CRP 8, p. 4.

28. The *Annual Report*, published by the "Association for Palestinian
Economic, Social and Development Cooperation," based in Geneva,
Switzerland, put the Palestinian population at 4,900,000. The report said
that 59% of the Palestinian population lives outside the boundaries of
historical or "mandatory" Palestine. Inside the Occupied Territories there
are two million Palestinians among which there are 894,000 in the West
Bank, 536,000 in the Gaza Strip and 608,000 in pre-1967 Israel. See *WAFA*,
February 2, 1986, pp. 4-5.

29. To demonstrate the importance to the Palestinian people of channel-
ing these funds, it suffices to mention that during seven months, $250 million
were allowed to enter the territories from "Jordan and the Arab states." Statement made by Yitzhak Rabin in the Israeli Knesset. *Israeli Radio*, March
16, 1986, quoted in: *Al-Rasd*, a bulletin published by the PLO Planning

Center on the Israeli organs of the mass media, No. 34, March 20, 1986, p. 21.

30. Unless otherwise indicated, the information in this section draws heavily on information supplied especially for this study by Mr. Abdul Rahman Bseisso, Director of the Information Department of the PRCS, based in Nicosia, Cyprus, during the month of March 1986.

31. Hamid, *Resolutions*, pp. 146-7.

32. Other studies have different estimates of the number of institutions run by the PRCS. Most of these studies have been researched before the Israeli invasion of Lebanon in 1982. See the excellent study mentioned earlier by Cheryl Rubenberg, particularly pp. 20-27 and 63-66.

33. Rubenberg, p. 23.

34. This section draws heavily on information supplied by the main office of the Society in Amman, Jordan, especially supplied for the purpose of this study on March 22, 1986.

35. Rubenberg, p. 55.

36. Israel is not only usurping Palestinian culture, it has also been usurping the cultures of other countries, such as Egypt. See interview with Egyptian musician Faraj Antari on Israel's usurpation of Egyptian and Palestinian music in *Al Yom Assabeh*, an Arab weekly magazine published in Paris, March 10, 1986, pp. 32-33.

37. "The Report of the General Administration to the Third Congress," Proceedings of SAMED's Third Congress, July 17-20, 1985, Amman, Jordan, in *SAMED*, a monthly economic journal published in Arabic, Vol. VII, No. 57, September-October 1985, p. 32.

38. The speech of Abu 'Ala', Director General of SAMED, in SAMED proceedings, ibid, p. 19.

39. Ibid., p. 70.

40. "Opening address of Chairman Arafat to SAMED's Third Congress, in SAMED proceedings, ibid. p. 5.

41. Ibid., p. 22.

42. Ibid.

43. Ibid., p. 6. Chairman Arafat was talking in July 1985 at the height of the cooperation between the PLO and Jordan, following the signature of the Jordanian-PLO Accord on February 11, 1985.

44. Introduction to SAMED's 1968 Diary.

45. SAMED proceedings, op. cit. p. 22.

46. Ibid., p. 38.

47. Ibid., p. 25.

48. Ibid., p. 39.

49. Ibid., p. 7.

50. Ibid., p. 37.

51. Ibid., pp. 46-47.

52. Ibid., p. 50.

53. Ibid., p. 6.

54. Ibid., p. 88.

55. Ibid.

56. Brigadier Muhammed T. Al-Russan, *Collection of Penal Laws of the PLO, 1979* (Beirut: PLO, the Palestinian Revolutionary Judiciary Department, 1980). Second Edition published in Tunis by Al-Maghreb Al-Arabi Publication House, 1986, p. 346.

P L O STRUCTURE

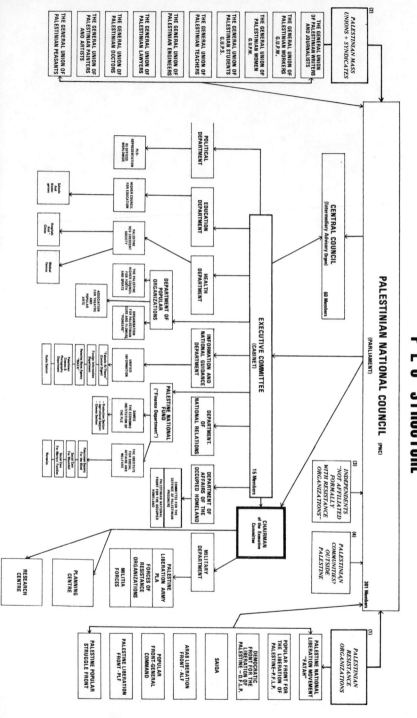